Disclaimer

The content provided in *This is TikTok: Your Complete Guide to Creating, Growing & Monetizing on TikTok* (hereinafter referred to as "the Book") is intended solely for educational and informational purposes. It is designed to assist readers in understanding the general principles, features, strategies, and monetization opportunities available on the TikTok platform, as understood at the time of writing.

While the author and publisher have made every effort to ensure the accuracy, currency, and reliability of the information presented herein, **TikTok and its features are dynamic, frequently updated, and subject to changes**. Therefore, readers should be aware that some content may become outdated or obsolete due to platform updates, feature discontinuations, changes to community guidelines, algorithm shifts, or new policy implementations by TikTok or its parent company, ByteDance Ltd.

No Affiliation with TikTok

This Book is an independent publication and is **not affiliated with, endorsed by, sponsored by, or officially connected to TikTok, ByteDance Ltd., or any of its subsidiaries**. All product names, logos, brands, and trademarks mentioned within this Book remain the property of their respective holders. Any use of these names, logos, or trademarks is for identification and reference purposes only and does not imply any association, approval, or sponsorship.

Earnings and Performance Disclaimer

The Book may discuss potential strategies and methods for growing a following, building engagement, and monetizing content on TikTok, including but not limited to: Creator Fund participation, brand partnerships, gifting, live stream features, promotional tools, and other income-generating programs. However, **the author makes no guarantees of specific outcomes or earnings**. Individual success on TikTok is influenced by a multitude of variables including, but not limited to, content quality, consistency, audience interaction, niche selection, trends, algorithmic behavior, marketing knowledge, and personal effort.

Any examples of income, performance, or audience growth cited in the Book are for illustrative purposes only and should not be interpreted as typical results or a promise of success. Your experience may differ significantly.

No Legal, Financial, or Professional Advice

Nothing in this Book should be considered as legal, financial, business, tax, or professional advice. While the Book touches on topics related to online monetization, promotional strategies, and brand collaboration, it does not substitute for professional consultation. Readers are encouraged to consult qualified professionals (such as lawyers, accountants, or business advisors) before making any legal or financial decisions, entering into contracts, or managing revenue streams related to content creation.

Book Description

Unlock the full potential of the world's fastest-growing platform — and turn scrolls into success.

Whether you're brand new to TikTok or ready to level up your presence, *This is TikTok: Your Complete Guide to Creating, Growing & Monetizing on TikTok* is your all-in-one playbook for building influence, connecting with audiences, and turning creativity into opportunity.

From setting up your first account to mastering LIVE features, brand collaborations, and monetization programs, this guide walks you through every essential feature, tool, and strategy available on the platform. You'll learn how to personalize your feed, create scroll-stopping content, harness the power of TikTok's editing suite, and grow a loyal community — all while understanding the systems that drive visibility, engagement, and income.

Inside, you'll discover:

- How to navigate the TikTok interface and customize your content feed

- Step-by-step guidance for shooting, editing, and publishing viral videos

- Powerful tools like Duets, Stitches, and Stories to boost creativity and reach

- Everything you need to know about TikTok LIVE, Creator Teams, and Co-Hosting

- In-depth insights into monetization options: Creator Fund, gifting, memberships, brand deals & more

- Pro-level tips on using analytics, TikTok Promote, and content calendars to grow strategically

- A breakdown of TikTok Studio, Live Studio, and advanced creator tools

- Community guidelines, platform safety, and account management best practices

Whether you're a creator, entrepreneur, marketer, or simply curious about how TikTok works, this book is your trusted roadmap to navigating the platform — and thriving in its vibrant, fast-moving ecosystem.

Create. Engage. Monetize. This is TikTok.

TABLE OF CONTENT

Mastering the App, Growing Your Presence, and Monetizing Your Creativity

Preface

"Don't make ads. Make TikToks."
   It's more than just a slogan — it's a fundamental shift in how we communicate, market, learn, and entertain in the digital age.

Over the past few years, TikTok has redefined the way people connect with content. It has turned ordinary users into household names. It has made viral moments out of mundane tasks. It has helped brands go from zero to sold out in a single weekend. And most of all, it has made content creation more accessible than ever — no studio, no fancy gear, no traditional training needed. Just an idea, a phone, and the courage to press record.

Yet, for many people — new users, aspiring creators, parents, business owners — TikTok can feel chaotic, overwhelming, or even intimidating.
That's where this book comes in.

🌑 Why This Guide Was Created

TikTok is a powerful platform, but it's also an ever-changing one. New features roll out weekly. Monetization tools shift. Guidelines get updated. What worked last month might not work this week. This guide was created to give you the confidence, clarity, and structure to keep up — and stay ahead.

This is not just a walkthrough of TikTok's features. It's a **comprehensive roadmap** for mastering the platform — from your very first post to long-term growth, monetization, and brand-building.

Whether you're an individual hoping to express yourself, a business owner looking for exposure, or a creator hoping to turn passion into profit — TikTok has space for you. And this book will show you exactly how to use it.

👤 Who This Book is For

This guide was written with **everyone** in mind. If you're:

- **A complete beginner**, wondering how to sign up or post your first video
- **A creator** hoping to increase your followers, get on the FYP, and explore new content strategies
- **A parent**, looking to understand how TikTok works and how to protect your teen
- **A business or brand**, aiming to leverage TikTok for visibility, engagement, and sales
- **An experienced user**, curious about deeper features like LIVE gifts, Creator Marketplace, or Shop integrations
   Then this book is for you.

You don't need to be a tech genius or social media expert — just curious, open, and ready to learn.

What You'll Learn Inside

This guide is broken into seven sections, each focused on helping you grow, create, earn, and thrive on the platform:

- **Part I** covers getting started — setting up your account, navigating the interface, and mastering privacy & security.
- **Part II** dives into creating TikToks — from using filters and effects to editing and publishing content.
- **Part III** explores the world of **TikTok LIVE**, including multi-guest lives, battles, gifting systems, and moderation.
- **Part IV** focuses on **membership systems**, rewards, gifting tiers, and how to level up your presence and income.
- **Part V** breaks down TikTok's **Creator Programs** — including Creator Next, Creator Marketplace, the Rewards Program, and affiliate opportunities.
- **Part VI** focuses on analytics, activity tracking, safety tools, and platform policies.
- **Part VII** includes bonus tips, a full glossary, icon and badge reference charts, FAQs, and platform updates.

This guide is designed to grow with you — whether you're here to build a career, promote a product, share your art, teach, entertain, or just have fun.

TikTok is Evolving — and So is This Book

At the time of this writing, TikTok's features are more advanced than ever — but that won't be true for long. The app evolves rapidly, often silently. New monetization tools, interface changes, and regional updates roll out constantly. This guide has been created with that flexibility in mind: it's modular, searchable, and easy to update.

We'll refer often to version numbers, feature availability by region, and platform updates to ensure you're getting the most current and accurate guidance possible.

✦ Final Words

TikTok is more than just a platform — it's a canvas, a community, and a launchpad. What you do with it is up to you. Whether you're documenting your life, growing your brand, building a business, or just having fun — your presence on TikTok can matter.

This book will help you:

- Show up confidently
- Create with purpose
- Understand how TikTok works under the hood
- And turn creativity into opportunity

So, flip the page, tap into your potential, and let's begin.
Because your first—or next—viral moment is waiting.

Welcome to TikTok. Let's master it together.

Chapter 1. Creating and Setting Up an Account

Getting started on TikTok is quick and user-friendly, but it's worth doing it right from the beginning — especially if you plan to grow your presence, protect your privacy, or unlock creator features later on.

1.1 Downloading the TikTok App

- Available on the **App Store (iOS)** and **Google Play Store (Android)**
- Look for the official app by *TikTok Pte. Ltd.*

1.2 Signing Up : You can sign up using:

- **Phone number**
- **Email address**
- **Apple ID / Google / Facebook / Instagram / Twitter**

🔒 *Tip: Use an email or phone number you'll always have access to — it makes account recovery easier.*

1.3 Choosing a Username

- Make it **memorable** and **brandable**
- Keep it **consistent** across platforms if you're growing a brand

1.4 Setting Up Your Profile

- Upload a **profile picture** or **Avatar**
- Add a **bio** — you can use emojis, hashtags, or even Linktree links
- Include your **website link** (unlocked after a certain follower count or switching to a business/creator account)

1.5 Choosing Your Account Type

You can switch between:

- **Personal Account** – Default for all users
- **Creator Account** – For content creators looking to grow
- **Business Account** – For brands and businesses (includes more analytics + ad tools)

⚒ To switch: Go to **Settings → Manage Account → Switch to Creator/Business**

Under Account Information , you will find your phone , email and region (Region is set based on time and place of registration)

☐ How to Perform ID Verification on TikTok

"Verification unlocks access — from monetization to advanced tools."

TikTok requires **identity verification** to access key features like monetization tools (e.g., TikTok Shop, LIVE gifting, Creator Rewards), protect accounts from impersonation, and ensure compliance with regional laws.

Verifying your ID is a **one-time process** that usually takes just a few minutes, but it must be done correctly to avoid delays or rejection.

■ When ID Verification Is Required:

- Applying to TikTok Shop (as a seller or affiliate)
- Enabling LIVE Gifts or Creator Rewards
- Accessing age-restricted features (e.g., going LIVE)
- Joining the Creator Marketplace
- Verifying a business account
- Appealing account bans (in some cases)

➡️ How to Submit Your ID for Verification

1. **Open the TikTok App** and go to your profile.
2. Tap the ☰ **menu** (top-right corner) → **Settings and Privacy**
3. Scroll down and tap **Account > Identity Verification** (this may appear under "Creator Tools" or "Business Suite" depending on your account type).
4. Choose your verification type:

   - **Personal Account**: For individual creators
   - **Business Account**: For companies, brands, or organizations

5. Upload a **valid government-issued ID**:

   - Passport
   - Driver's license
   - National ID card (both sides if applicable)

6. ● Ensure your name, photo, and date of birth are clear and match your TikTok profile.
7. Follow the prompts to take a **selfie** or **face scan** for identity confirmation.
8. Submit and wait for the review. Verification usually takes **up to 48 hours**, but can be faster.

● Tips to Ensure a Smooth Verification Process

- Use a **well-lit area** when scanning your document
- Avoid glare or shadows on your ID
- Make sure all text is **readable and not cropped**
- Submit **original documents only** (no photocopies or edits)
- Your **TikTok display name doesn't need to match**, but your **registered info must**

▲ If Your Verification Fails

If your ID is rejected:

- You'll receive a notification with a reason
- You may re-submit with corrected documentation
- If the issue persists, contact TikTok Support via:

  ○ **Profile > ☰ > Settings > Report a Problem**
  ○ Or through **TikTok Shop/Seller Center support** if verifying for commerce

📌 **Final Note:** ID verification is **private and secure**. TikTok uses encryption   to protect your personal data and does not publicly display verification status (unlike blue-check verification).

Chapter 2: Navigating the TikTok Interface

Once your account is created and your profile is set up, the next step is to get comfortable with the TikTok interface — your command center for everything you'll watch, post, or manage. Whether you're just here to consume content or planning to become a creator, understanding TikTok's navigation is key to making the most of the platform.

The layout may vary slightly between devices, regions, or account types, but the core structure includes a series of main tabs typically found at the bottom and top of your screen.

2.1 ◆ Home Tab

This is the default tab you land on when opening the app. It's split into two feeds:

2.2 ◆ *For You Page (FYP)*

The For You Page is a **customized feed** generated by TikTok's algorithm. It shows content based on:

- What you watch (especially to completion)
- What you like, share, or comment on
- Who you follow
- Which content you search for or engage with

Expect this feed to adapt over time as TikTok learns your preferences. For many creators and brands, getting on users' FYPs is the ultimate goal — **it's how content goes viral.**

2.3 ◆ *Following Tab*

Switch to this feed to only see content from people you follow. It's ideal for keeping up with creators you like, friends, or niche accounts.

> 🗨 *Pro Tip:* Tap and hold on any video to bring up the "Not Interested" option or to save it for later. These interactions help fine-tune your FYP and future recommendations. This will also bring up the following options :report ,save video ,add to story,captions, clear display, playback speed,promote and Why this video (which you can use to fine tune your FYP)

2.4 🔍 Search (Discover/Explore) Tab

Depending on your version of TikTok or region, this tab may appear as either **"Discover"** or **"Explore"**, but its function is mostly the same: it's TikTok's search and content discovery hub.

- ◆ Key Features:

- Search for **videos, users, sounds, hashtags, effects**

- View trending hashtags and topics
- Get access to content across different categories (education, food, gaming, etc.)

This is especially helpful when you're trying to find niche content, check if a trend is still active, or discover new creators in your area of interest.

> 💡 *Search by sound* to find all videos that use a particular audio clip — a powerful tool for trend-jumping and content ideas.

2.5 ✏ Experimental Tabs (**May Appear for Select Users**)

TikTok frequently tests new layouts and features. Depending on your engagement, location, or account type, you may see one or more **optional or special-purpose tabs** appear alongside the core ones. These include:

2.6 🔬 STEM Tab

The STEM tab is a dedicated space for educational and informative content. You'll find:

- Science experiments
- Engineering demonstrations
- Explainer videos in technology, health, space, chemistry, physics, and more

This feed is often curated and fact-checked, particularly in partnership with reputable educational organizations. It's perfect for learners, educators, and creators in knowledge-sharing spaces.

> 👊 *STEM creators benefit from niche exposure here, as their content avoids getting lost in mainstream entertainment feeds.*

2.7 🛍 SHOP Tab

TikTok Shop is TikTok's built-in e-commerce ecosystem. The **Shop tab** connects users to:

- Live sales events
- Product listings
- Influencer affiliate promotions
- Personalized product recommendations based on your browsing and purchase history

If you interact with shopping content, watch unboxings, or follow creator-sellers, TikTok may enable this tab for your account.
 Business and Creator accounts using TikTok Shop can manage product integration directly from here.

🛒 *Think of this as TikTok meets Amazon, with one-click discovery and checkout all in-app.*

2.8 ● EXPLORE Tab

The Explore tab is TikTok's experimental replacement for Discover. It segments content into **topic categories** like:

- Food

- Comedy

- Travel

- Fitness

- Gaming

- Style/Fashion

- Life Hacks

This layout mimics YouTube and Instagram's explore experiences, allowing users to **deep dive into interest-based themes** without relying on hashtags alone.

🔎 *Explore tabs are often tested with highly engaged users or those who follow a wide variety of creators.*

2.9 👤 Profile Tab

Your Profile tab is your personal space on TikTok — it's how others see you, and how you manage your own content. Here, you can:

- View all videos you've posted (public and private)
- See your **Drafts** (saved videos not yet published)
- Track follower and following counts
- View videos you've liked (if visible), and access your saved sounds, effects, and playlists
- Edit your bio, change your profile picture/video, add social links, and monitor your content performance

- At the top of your profile, you'll find access to:
- **LIVE Center** (if eligible)
- Creator Tools
- **TikTok Shop dashboard** (if you're enrolled)
- Your profile's **QR code** for easy sharing

Everything you build, create, or engage with funnels through this tab — treat it like your content resume.

📌 Summary: What You See May Depend on You

Tab	Purpose	May Be Hidden or Shown Based On
Home	Primary video feed (FYP & Following)	Standard for all users
Discover/Search	Find users, hashtags, sounds	Some accounts see "Explore" instead
Inbox	Notifications & messages	Standard for all users
Profile	View and manage your account	Standard for all users
STEM	Educational feed	Appears based on interest/activity
SHOP	In-app shopping & product links	Shown to users who engage with shopping
EXPLORE	Topic-based discovery	Part of A/B testing or new layout rollouts

Chapter 3: Personalizing Your Feed

"Your TikTok feed should feel like it was made for you — because it is."

3.1 🗨 How the TikTok Algorithm Works

At the core of TikTok's experience is its **powerful recommendation engine** — better known as the For You Page (FYP). It's what sets TikTok apart from other social platforms. Instead of showing you only content from people you follow, TikTok shows you what it thinks you'll *want to see*, based on an ever-evolving understanding of your behavior.

Here's what the algorithm takes into account:

- **Watch Time** – Videos you watch all the way through are highly prioritized

- **Rewatches** – If you replay a video, TikTok assumes it's especially valuable
- **Likes & Comments** – These signal your approval and interest
- **Shares & Saves** – Engagement beyond the app (DMs, reposts, saving to favorites)
- **Search Activity** – What you actively look for matters
- **Post Interactions** – If you follow or interact with the creator after a video
- **Hashtags & Sounds** – What kind of content you're drawn to thematically
- **Device, Language & Location** – Your settings help TikTok suggest local or language-based content

> 💡 *Unlike Instagram or Facebook, TikTok doesn't prioritize followers — it prioritizes engagement and interest.*

3.2 🐾 What Shapes Your Feed

Every interaction is data. Even passive ones. If you scroll quickly past a video, TikTok registers disinterest. If you pause for a few seconds — even without liking or commenting — TikTok interprets it as curiosity.

Some less obvious factors:

- **Time of day usage** – When you watch affects what you see
- **Video length preferences** – Do you prefer short clips or 3-minute deep dives?
- **Sound preferences** – TikTok may adjust recommendations based on audio genres
- **New vs. returning users** – New accounts may see broader, more trend-heavy content

This creates a feedback loop. The more you engage with a certain type of content, the more TikTok shows you similar videos — until your feed feels hyper-personalized.

3.3 ⚫ How to Train the Algorithm to Work for You

TikTok doesn't just *learn* what you like — it allows you to *teach* it.

⬛ Do This:

- **Like, share, and comment** on content you want more of
- **Watch full videos**, especially ones you find valuable or entertaining
- **Save** videos to Favorites (long press > tap the bookmark icon)
- **Follow creators** who consistently post content in your interest
- **Explore similar hashtags or audio clips** for niche discovery

⬛ Avoid This:

- **Letting the app idle while distracted** (TikTok may track watch time on irrelevant videos)
- **Engaging with content you dislike just to "correct" it** — use "Not Interested" instead
- **Scrolling passively for long periods without interacting** (this reduces your signal strength)
  📌 *You are in full control. Be mindful, and TikTok becomes the most custom platform on your phone.*

3.4 🛠 Using TikTok Tools to Fine-Tune Your Feed

TikTok offers several built-in features that allow you to curate your experience:

🖊 *Clear Watch History*

- Go to: **Settings → Activity Center → Watch History , up to 180 days**
- You can view or clear your history to reset what TikTok shows you

👎 *Not Interested Option*

- Long-press on a video and tap **"Not Interested"**
- You can even **hide content from certain creators** or **mute specific sounds**

⬛ *Content Preferences*

- Located in Settings > Content Preferences

- You can select or block content by:

  - **Language**
  - **Topics**
  - **Refresh your FYP**
  - **Mute words**

- Captions/subtitles
- **Restricted Mode** (for filtering mature content)

3.5 🔍 Leveraging the Search & Explore Tab

The **Search bar** is one of TikTok's most underused personalization tools.

Try these:

- Search for niche terms like "dark academia outfit inspo" or "easy 5-minute breakfast"
- Tap on the **sounds** or **hashtags** used in top-performing results
- Watch multiple videos in a niche cluster to trigger algorithmic shifts

You'll often see your FYP begin to reflect your searches within a few hours — or even minutes.

We talk about creator search insight later.

3.6 🎧 Favoriting & Interacting with Sounds

TikTok's engine heavily prioritizes **audio behavior**, including:

- Which sounds you listen to repeatedly
- Whether you favorite or use a sound
  How long you engage with videos using certain tracks

How to favorite a sound:

1. Tap the spinning **record icon** on the bottom right of any video
2. Tap **Add to Favorites**
3. You'll now find this sound under your "Saved" tab in your profile

   🎶 *Trending sounds not only boost your own content — they also tell TikTok what themes or moods you enjoy consuming.*

3.7 💡 Feed Behavior for Niche Users

If you're someone who's deeply into one or more niches — say BookTok, FinTok, FoodTok, or AnimeTok — here's how to signal that interest clearly:

- Use **search terms** related to that niche
- **Comment and engage** with niche creators
- Follow multiple creators from the same space

- Participate in challenges, duets, and trends relevant to the community

Before long, your FYP will resemble an insider feed of your niche's best and most popular posts.

3.8 ● How TikTok Adjusts Over Time

TikTok doesn't "lock" your interests. If your behavior changes, so will your feed. In fact, TikTok regularly tests your behavior by injecting a few videos outside your usual scope. If you engage with them, it may start nudging your feed in that direction.

To manage this:

- Be consistent in the type of content you engage with
- Use the **"Not Interested"** option liberally to keep your feed clean
- Regularly check your Watch and Comment History to review your digital footprint

3.9 ■ Building a Feed That Inspires Creation

If you're planning to post or go LIVE, your feed should also be your **content laboratory** — a source of inspiration, trends, and tactics.

Set goals like:

- Following at least 5 creators in your niche
- Saving 3–5 videos daily that make you say: "I can do this"
  Observing post structure: hook, content, and call to action

   ● *Your feed should not only entertain you — it should inspire you to create content you enjoy making.*

■ Summary Checklist: Personalizing Your Feed

Action	Why It Matters
Watch full videos	Boosts relevance
Like, comment, and follow	Strengthens algorithmic signals
Save videos, sounds, effects	Influences feed and creation inspiration
Use "Not Interested"	Filters unwanted content
Explore niche topics via search	Expands and focuses your feed

| Favorite trending sounds | Aligns your interests with future trends |
| Monitor Watch History | Keeps your signal clean and targeted |

Ready to shape your TikTok experience?

Once your feed reflects your personality, interests, and goals — TikTok becomes more than just an app. It becomes your creative canvas.

Chapter 4: Settings & Privacy Essentials

"Your TikTok experience is only as powerful as the controls you understand."

TikTok isn't just about content and trends — it's also a complex system filled with privacy settings, notification tools, screen time tracking, and app optimization features. This chapter will walk you through the **Settings & Privacy panel**, section by section, to help you use the app with confidence, safety, and intention.

Access this menu by tapping on your **Profile** → ☰ **(Menu/three-line icon)** → **Settings and privacy**.

⚙ 4.1 Navigating the Settings Menu

The settings menu is divided into multiple sections, including (order may vary):

- **Account Management**
- **Privacy**
- **Security**
- **Content & Display**
- **Notifications**
- **App Behavior** (data, storage, language)
- **Family Pairing & Safety**
- **Support**

Let's break them down.

👤 4.2 Account Management

Under **Manage Account**, you'll find the tools to:

- Change your **email**, **phone number**, or **password**
- Switch or log out of accounts
- Enable or disable **account verification** (Creator/Business)
- Manage **Orders**, **TikTok Shop**, and **Account Info**

  🗨 *If you plan to monetize or collaborate with brands, make sure your info here is accurate and verified.*

🔒 4.3 Privacy Settings

This section gives you full control over how others interact with your content.

Key privacy features include:

📌 Profile Visibility

- **Private Account** – Only approved followers can view your content
- **Suggest Your Account to Others** – Appear in friend recommendations

💬 Interaction Controls

- **Comments** – Everyone, followers only, or no one
- **Mentions & Tags** – Control who can tag or mention you
- **Direct Messages** – Fully disabled, followers only, or everyone
- **Duets & Stitches** – Choose who can remix your videos
- **Downloads** – Enable or disable video downloads
- **Favorite Sounds, Videos, and Effects** – Keep your saved content private or public
- **Following and Followers Lists** – Choose visibility of these tabs

🔒 *Every creator should customize these to match their comfort level — especially if younger audiences are involved.*

🛡 4.4 Security & Login Protection

Found under **Security and Permissions** , this section helps protect your TikTok account from unauthorized access.

Key options include:

- **Two-Step Verification** – Highly recommended! Adds a layer of security
- **Manage Devices** – See which phones or computers have access to your account
- **Security Alerts** – Get notified of login attempts
- **Save Login Info** – Toggle on/off for ease or enhanced protection
- **Help Friends Recover Accounts** – TikTok allows account recovery through mutual friends
- **Apps and Services permissions** : to view apps that are linked to your tiktok.

⬛ 4.5 Content & Display Preferences

TikTok allows you to shape not only *what* you see but also *how* you see it.

🚶 Accessibility

- Font size, contrast, screen reader support

● Language Preferences

- Preferred language for videos
- Interface and subtitle languages

🎥 Playback Settings

- **Open TikTok on mute** (default behavior)
- Auto-play options
  Video brightness (toggle based on time of day)

Screen Time give you information on how much time spent on tiktok daily or weekly , you can customize this to receive notifications .

🔔 4.6 Notification Center

This section controls all your **push** and **in-app notifications** — and it's more customizable than most users realize.

Notification categories include:

- Likes
- Comments
- New followers
- Mentions & tags
- TikTok LIVE activity
- Recommendations
- Suggested creators
- Promotional updates

You can also set a **notification schedule** to mute TikTok alerts at night or during work hours.

> ● *TikTok can be addictive — use this section to reduce digital noise and reclaim your focus.*

🧹 4.7 Freeing Up Space & Data Use

Found under **"Cache & Cellular"** or **"Data Saver"**, these settings help TikTok run more smoothly.

Tools include:

- **Free Up Space** – Clear cached video files, drafts, search history
- **Data Saver Mode** – Reduces mobile data usage by lowering video resolution
- **Offline Videos** – See which clips are stored locally and delete them

⚙ *If TikTok starts lagging or crashing, this is where to troubleshoot.*

👥 4.8 Family Pairing

For parents and guardians, TikTok includes a **Family Pairing mode** that allows oversight of a teen's account.

Features include:

- **Screen time controls**
- **Restricted content filters**
- **Limit who can message or follow Private account enforcement**
- **View content history and activity**

Family Pairing requires syncing two TikTok accounts — the parent's and the teen's — and can be disabled at any time.

> 🧩 *Look for this section especially if your child is under 16 — it's a vital part of the TikTok safety system.*

⬛ 4.9 Support, Terms & Community Rules

At the bottom of the Settings menu, you'll find:

- TikTok's **Community Guidelines**
- **Help Center**
- **Feedback & bug reporting**
- **Ad personalization settings**
- Legal and Terms of Service

This section is where you'll go if:

- You want to report harassment or abuse
- You believe your video was unfairly removed
- You need to appeal a content decision or account restriction

■ Summary: Mastering Settings & Privacy

Feature	Purpose	Recommended Use
Manage Account	Update login info & verify access	Keep everything secure and up to date
Privacy Settings	Control how others interact with you	Use strict settings for teen accounts
Security & Devices	Prevent hacks or login leaks	Enable 2FA and review devices monthly
Notifications	Limit distractions	Customize by content type
Free Up Space	Optimize app performance	Use weekly or after heavy usage
Family Pairing	Supervise younger users	Essential for under-18 creators
Support Tools	Report problems or learn more	Use as needed for assistance

🔒 **Ready to control your TikTok experience?**

Now that your app is set up and secure, you're ready to explore deeper content tools and creation strategies.

🎥 Setting Up Two-Step Verification

Two-Step Verification (also called 2FA) is one of the most effective ways to protect your TikTok account from unauthorized access. When enabled, it adds an extra layer of security by requiring both your password **and** a secondary verification method — such as a code sent to your phone or email — whenever you or someone else tries to log in from a new device.

Here's how to set it up:

1. Open TikTok and go to your **Profile**.

2. Tap the ☰ **(Menu)** icon in the top right.

3. Select **Settings and privacy** → **Security** → **Two-step verification**.

4. Choose your preferred verification methods:

    ○ **SMS (text message)**

    ○ **Email**

    ○ **Password** (fallback method)

You can choose one or more of these for backup access. TikTok will send a verification code to your selected method when needed — for example, during logins from new devices or when performing sensitive actions like password changes.

> ● *Tip: For maximum protection, enable both SMS and email verification. This ensures you'll have a backup even if you lose access to one method.*

Once set up, Two-Step Verification works silently in the background, offering peace of mind every time you open the app.

Verification on TikTok gives your account the **blue checkmark badge**, signaling that you are a **notable creator, public figure, brand, or entity**. It builds **trust**, increases your visibility in search, and can improve opportunities with brand deals or TikTok features.

What TikTok Looks For:

- Authenticity – You are who you say you are
- Uniqueness – One account per person or brand
- Activity – Consistent content and growth
- Notability – You are featured in news, are publicly recognized, or have an online presence
- Security – You have 2-Step Verification enabled

How to Request Verification:

> Note: TikTok does not offer a self-serve "Request Verification" form like Instagram. Instead, they manually verify accounts or respond to inquiries from media partners.

However, here's how to **optimize for verification**:

1. **Enable Two-Step Verification** (Chapter 4)
2. **Use your real name** or brand name in your profile
3. **Link a verified YouTube, Instagram, or Facebook account**
4. **Post consistently and engage regularly**
5. **Get external media coverage** (blogs, news, interviews)
6. **Collaborate with other verified creators**

If you meet eligibility, you may be **contacted by TikTok** or your account may be verified automatically.

Chapter 5: Creating TikTok Videos

"Everyone starts with zero followers. What matters is pressing record."

TikTok makes content creation accessible to everyone — whether you're a first-time user or a seasoned creator. With just a few taps, you can record, edit, and publish videos that reach millions. But to create videos that **stand out**, you'll want to understand the tools TikTok offers and how to use them with intention.

In this chapter, you'll learn:

- How to start a video from scratch
- How to use filters, effects, and music
- Editing tools before and after recording
- Best practices for your first few videos

5.1 Starting a New Video

To begin recording:

1. Tap the ✚ **(plus icon)** in the center of the navigation bar.
2. This opens TikTok's camera and editing suite.

You'll now see a number of options on screen — let's break them down.

Camera Controls:

- **Flip** – Switch between front and rear cameras.
- **Speed** – Record in real-time, slow motion, or time-lapse.
- **Timer** – Set a countdown (3s or 10s) before recording starts.
- **Flash** – Toggle light for low-light settings.
- **Filters & Effects** – Apply visual styles or augmented reality features.

5.2 Adding Music or Sounds

TikTok is built on sound — music drives trends, sets the tone, and helps videos get discovered.

To add a sound:

- Tap **"Add sound"** at the top of the screen.

- Browse trending audio or search by keyword.
- Tap the **bookmark icon** to save for later.

🎧 *Tip: Using trending sounds can improve your chances of appearing on the For You Page.*

You can also use your own voice, record ambient sound, or do voiceovers (explained in 5.4).

🧩 5.3 Uploading Instead of Recording

If you've already created content outside TikTok, you can upload it:

- Tap the **"Upload"** button (bottom right of the record screen).
- Choose videos (or photos) from your phone gallery.
- Trim, crop, reorder, and edit using TikTok's built-in editor.

▪️ *Many creators film externally, edit with apps like CapCut or VN, then upload to TikTok for final polishing.*

✂️ 5.4 Editing Your Video (Before and After Recording)

TikTok lets you edit **before, during, and after** you record. Here's what to expect:

Pre-Recording:

- **Select duration** (15s, 60s, 3m, or 10m)
- **Set up Green Screen, Filters, or AR Effects**
- **Enable Beauty Mode** or "Enhance" options

Post-Recording:

- **Trim clips** or split into scenes
- Add **captions** (automatic or manual)
- Use **voice effects** or **voiceover tools**
- Place **text overlays** with timing controls
- Add **stickers**, emojis, or GIFs
- Choose a **cover photo** and add a title

🛠️ *The editing tools may look simple, but they're incredibly powerful — experiment with them to develop your unique style.*

🗨 5.5 Tips for Your First Few Videos

Everyone's first video is rough — and that's okay. The goal is to **start creating consistently**. Here are a few tips:

- **Use popular trends** to ease in — lip-syncs, challenges, or funny audios
- **Keep videos under 30 seconds** to maximize retention
- **Start with strong hooks** ("You won't believe this…" or "Here's a quick tip…")
- **Engage with your audience** in captions or comments
- **Don't stress over perfection** — TikTok rewards authenticity

✏ *Your first 10–20 videos are experiments. The more you post, the faster you'll improve and grow.*

We have a chapter desiccated to content creation.

...[Previous Content]...

■ 5.6: Understanding the TikTok Point System

"Engagement isn't just feedback — it's your fuel for reach."

TikTok's algorithm is famously secretive, but through observed behavior and creator analytics, many experts agree that the platform operates on a **point-based engagement system**. This system helps determine how widely a video will be shown, starting with a small audience and expanding only if engagement signals are strong enough.

✏ How the Point System Works

Every video uploaded to TikTok is first shown to a **"trial audience"**, typically around **300 viewers**. Based on how that group interacts with the video, TikTok decides whether to boost it further.

To do so, TikTok assigns **point values to different types of viewer engagement**. These points accumulate to a score that determines whether the video passes the "trial phase."

■ Estimated Engagement Points:

Action	Point Value
Like	1 point
Comment	2 points
Repost/Share	3 points
Full Video Watch (100%)	4 points
Rewatch (plays again)	5 points

⬤ **Threshold for Expansion**: Once a video hits **50 engagement points**, TikTok begins showing it to a wider audience segment.

This expansion phase can repeat at increasing tiers, allowing successful videos to go **from a few hundred views to hundreds of thousands or more** in a matter of hours.

🚀 Why This Matters

Unlike platforms where follower count drives exposure, TikTok's For You Page algorithm relies heavily on **engagement performance** — meaning **anyone can go viral** if their content hits the right metrics early.

🧠 Algorithmic Influence:

- The **more points** your video accumulates, the **higher** it ranks in TikTok's discovery engine

- High early engagement often leads to placement in:

  - The "For You" feed

- Relevant hashtag pages

- Trending topic sections

■ *Videos that re-circulate through rewatches and shares are more likely to sustain momentum, which can **trigger multiple waves of reach**.*

⚒ Strategies to Increase Engagement Points

To maximize your video's point potential and performance:

🎧 1. Create Hook-Worthy Content

The first 1–3 seconds are everything. Use bold visuals, strong text overlays, or an unexpected action to stop scrolling and hook interest.

■ 2. Design Loopable Videos

Structure your video so the ending connects logically with the beginning. This makes viewers rewatch without realizing it, **earning rewatch points** and reinforcing watch time.

💬 3. Encourage Audience Interaction

- Ask a simple question in the caption

- Say "Comment your answer below" or "Double-tap if you agree"

- Promote sharing: "Send this to someone who needs to hear it"

Every action counts toward the total score.

🎶 4. Use Trending Sounds and Hashtags

Align your content with:

- Viral sounds

- Niche or trending hashtags

- Current challenges

This increases discoverability and invites viewers already engaging with those trends.

◣ 5. Optimize Video Length and Pacing

Shorter videos (8–20 seconds) tend to perform better early, especially if they pack a punch. Fast cuts, captions, and focused ideas help retain viewers until the end.

■ Section Summary: TikTok's Point System Strategy

Element	Benefit
Trial Audience	Starts video exposure with 300 users
Engagement Points	Determines expansion potential
50-Point Threshold	Required to unlock broader distribution
Rewatch & Retention	Highest value metric for algorithm performance
Strategic Content Design	Increases engagement and boosts point accrual

*Understanding the point system gives you a strategic edge. It's not just about creativity — it's about **engineering content to perform**.*

■ *Coming up next: Section 5.7 – Analytics Breakdown: How to Track Performance Like a Pro*

→■ Ready to Publish?

Once you're happy with your video:

1. Tap **Next**
2. Add a **caption**, hashtags, and mentions
3. Choose visibility: Public, Friends, or Private
4. Allow comments, Duets, and Stitches (optional)
5. Tap **Post** — or save to **Drafts** if you want to come back later

Chapter 6: TikTok Editing Tools Explained

"Your creativity, plus the right tools, equals unlimited potential."

✗ Overview

Creating standout videos on TikTok isn't about having expensive gear — it's about using **in-app tools strategically**. From video filters to sound effects and interactive overlays, TikTok provides a highly flexible creative suite. When used well, these tools can dramatically increase **retention, shares, and follower growth**.

This expanded chapter now includes:

- Pro tips for visual storytelling
- Shortcuts and hidden editing features

- Account verification overview

Let's dive deeper into each toolset and then explore how verification helps elevate your content and creator status.

✦ 6.1 Filters & Effects

- Filters

    - **Before recording**: Tap "Filters" on the right side of the recording screen.
    - **After recording**: Tap "Adjust Clips" → "Filters" to apply post-production looks.

Some creators use the same filter in every video to build a **recognizable aesthetic** — similar to using presets on Instagram.

Recommended Filters:

- *G6* – Neutral tone for vlogs
- *Brew* – Warm lighting for food/coffee content
- *F4* – High contrast for fashion edits

- Effects

Use effects in **three stages**:

1. **Before recording** – Real-time overlays
2. **During recording** – Layer new effects between clips

3. **After recording** – Add interactive or AR elements (via "Effects" under post-edit menu)

🎭 *Popular effects change weekly — check the "Trending" tab regularly to stay relevant.*

📱 6.2 Text & Captions

Text is more than decoration — it's part of your **narrative**. Use it to:

- Reinforce key messages
- Deliver punchlines
- Subtitle voice overs or speech

Style tips:

- Keep fonts consistent across your content for recognizability.
- Use **bold text with background** for accessibility.
- Animate text entry/exit using "Set Duration" and stagger text boxes to follow the video pace.

⚫ *Text should appear just before the viewer needs it — not after.*

🎧 6.3 Sound Editing, Voiceover & Audio Tips

🔊 Mixing Audio

- Tap the **"Volume"** button after recording to adjust:

    - Original video sound
    - Added sound/music volume

🎤 Voiceover Tips

- Use voiceover for:

    - Tutorial steps
    - Product commentary
    - Comedic narration
    - Storytime content

Make sure to **record in a quiet space** and **speak clearly**, or add auto-captions afterward.

▌ Hidden Audio Tips:

- Use the **"Sound Sync"** feature (only available on multi-clip uploads) to let TikTok automatically time your cuts to a song's beat.

- Add trending sounds **at low volume** underneath your narration to boost discoverability.

🧩 6.4 Layering Effects: Green Screen, Dupe, PIP

TikTok's layering tools can give you **film-style results**, even on your phone.

Green Screen (Pro Use Cases):

- Background storytelling (vacations, movie posters, reaction images)
- Education (charts, slideshows, news breakdowns)
- Content recycling (use your own previous posts as backgrounds!)

Split/Clone Tools:

- Film multiple clips in the same outfit with different expressions or lines
- Use **timing + layout** to make it look like you're interacting with yourself

Picture-in-Picture (PIP):

- Great for **reaction videos**, screen tutorials, or showcasing products while talking.

🎭 6.5 Stickers, Emojis & Interactive Layers

Stickers aren't just cute — they're strategic.

Try this:

- Use **"Follow me" arrows** to point at your handle
- Add **timer stickers** to create urgency in promos
- Include a **"new post" arrow** in your profile video preview

When to use:

- During calls to action
- At punchline moments
- To visually guide the viewer's eye across the screen

    🔥 *Minimalist design = higher retention. Don't overload your visuals.*

💡 6.6 Drafts, Post Scheduling & Batch Editing

Drafts are your **pre-post production studio**. Use them to:

- Batch-create content when you're in a creative mood
- Add captions later
- Save trends while waiting to jump in

To schedule a post (for Creator/Business accounts only):

- Record and edit your video
- On the posting screen, look for **"Schedule video"**
- Set the time and date

📓 *Posting at peak times (see Analytics in Chapter 20) can boost your reach dramatically.*

💬 Pro Tip: Creating a Personal Editing Style

Ask yourself:

- Do I want my videos to be calm and cinematic?
- Fast and high-energy?
- Text-heavy or music-driven?

Use:

- **Consistent fonts, colors, and filters**
- Reuse **certain effects or sounds** to create familiarity
- Experiment with **custom templates** in third-party apps

Your editing style can become your **brand signature** — something viewers associate with your content even before they see your username.

📕 With these tools, you're not just editing — you're storytelling, branding, and engaging all at once.

Chapter 7: Duets, Stitches & Stories

"TikTok isn't just about creating — it's about co-creating."

TikTok has redefined how content spreads online, and much of that comes from its **remix-friendly tools**: **Duet**, **Stitch**, and **Stories**. These features empower you to interact with other creators' videos, share your reactions, collaborate without planning, and participate in viral formats.

Whether you're building on someone's story, reacting to a hot take, or adding value to a tutorial, these tools make your content part of a larger dialogue — and can boost your visibility in the process.

🎤 7.1 What is a Duet?

A **Duet** places your video **side-by-side** with another user's, playing simultaneously. It's used for:

- **Reactions** and commentary
- **Singing/harmony videos**
- **Dance challenges**
- **Tutorials and responses**
- **Split-screen skits**

🔧 How to Duet:

1. Find a video you want to Duet.
2. Tap the **"Share" icon** → select **"Duet"**.
3. Choose your **layout** (side-by-side, top-bottom, green screen, react).
4. Record your side while the original video plays on the other side.
5. Edit, caption, and post like any other TikTok.

🧩 Layout Options:

- **Side-by-side** (classic)
- **Top and bottom**
- **React bubble** (your video in a circle overlaid on the original)
- **Green screen Duet** (use the other video as your background)
  🎭 *Duets are a powerful way to tap into trending content without needing to start from scratch.*

✂️ 7.2 What is a Stitch?

A **Stitch** lets you **clip and embed up to 5 seconds** of another user's video into the beginning of your own. You take their setup and provide the punchline, commentary, or continuation.

Used for:

- "Tell me you're a ___ without telling me you're a ___" videos
- **Story continuations**
- **Educational builds**
- **Discussions and debate**
- "Here's what they didn't mention..."

🔧 How to Stitch:

1. Find a video → tap **Share** → select **Stitch**
2. Use the slider to trim the first 1–5 seconds of their video
3. After their clip plays, record your continuation
4. Edit and post normally

🎤 *If Duets are conversations, Stitches are creative handoffs.*

📲 7.3 What are TikTok Stories?

TikTok Stories are temporary posts that disappear after **24 hours**, just like Instagram or Facebook Stories. They appear:

- On your **profile picture ring**
- In the **For You Page feed**
- Under the **Friends** tab (if you follow each other)

🧩 How to Post a Story:

1. Tap the **+ (Create)** button
2. Record a short video (up to 15 seconds) or upload one
3. Choose **"Post to Story"** instead of regular post

⬛ Story Features:

- You can **see who viewed** your story
- **Reply to stories** with DMs or emojis (if messaging is enabled)
- Use **poll stickers**, music, and effects like a normal post

💡 *Stories are a great way to post casual, behind-the-scenes, or in-progress content without disrupting your main feed.*

📽 7.4 Who Can Duet, Stitch, or See Stories?

You control it all under **Settings → Privacy → Interactions**:

- Allow or block **Duets/Stitches** on all your videos
- Toggle permissions **per post** during upload
- Stories are **public by default**, but **DM replies and view counts** depend on your privacy settings

⬤ *Not all videos are duet-able or stitchable — if the creator has restricted it, you'll see the option grayed out.*

7.5 Strategy: Using These Tools for Growth

💬 Be Intentional

- Duet videos that are already performing well (rising trends, viral moments)
- Stitch clips that prompt questions or open discussions
- Don't just react — **add value** (insight, humor, context, talent)

Boost Engagement

- Ask questions in your captions: "What do you think?" "Would you try this?"
- Duet your own videos to show updates, results, or audience reactions
- Reply to comments with a Stitch to keep the convo going

Drive Discoverability

- Use **trending audios and hashtags** in your Duets/Stitches
- Engage with creators in your **niche** or industry
- Tag collaborators and encourage followers to Stitch your original content

💬 *The best way to grow isn't to create in isolation — it's to create within conversation.*

7.6 Creator Tips & Pro Use Cases

- **Musicians**: Harmonize or do call-and-response Duets
- **Educators**: Stitch viral clips with expert commentary
- **Artists**: React to fan art or remix tutorials
- **Brands**: Duet user reviews or customer shout-outs

⬤ *Use these tools to build **community**, not just content.*

■ Summary: Remixing on TikTok

Tool	What It Does	Best Used For
Duet	Side-by-side video playback	Reactions, harmonies, challenges
Stitch	Clip the start of someone's video	Commentary, responses, storytelling
Stories	24-hour temporary content	Casual updates, behind-the-scenes moments

You're now equipped to **collaborate, remix, and participate** in TikTok's most social features — all while boosting your visibility and building creative momentum.

Awesome — now we enter one of the most powerful and dynamic aspects of TikTok: **LIVE streaming**.

Chapter 8: Going LIVE on TikTok

"When you go LIVE, you're not just posting — you're performing, connecting, and earning in real-time."

TikTok LIVE transforms how creators interact with their audiences. Whether you're showcasing your talent, answering questions, doing product demos, or just chatting with your followers, going LIVE gives you **instant visibility, direct feedback, and monetization potential** through gifts and incentives.

In this chapter, you'll learn:

- How to go LIVE and what you need to get started
- The different ways you can go LIVE (camera, voice chat, gaming, etc.)
- Best practices for planning and hosting a LIVE session
- How to maximize viewer engagement and earnings
- An overview of TikTok's LIVE tools, settings, and moderation features

---

→ 8.1 How to Go LIVE on TikTok

■ Eligibility Requirements:

- You must be **18 or older** to go LIVE
- You must have at least **1,000 followers (depending on Location , 150 followers is enough for some locations)**
- To **receive LIVE Gifts**, you must be **18+**

▲ If you don't see the LIVE button, you either don't meet the criteria or TikTok has temporarily restricted access due to guideline violations.

🎥 Steps to Go LIVE:

1. Open the TikTok app and tap the **"+" (Create)** button.
2. Swipe to the **LIVE** tab (next to the default video mode).
3. Add a **title** (up to 32 characters) — this is what users see when scrolling through LIVE recommendations.
4. Tap **"Go LIVE"** when ready.

8.2 Ways to Go LIVE

TikTok supports multiple LIVE formats — beyond just turning on your camera.

1. Device Camera (Standard LIVE)

- The classic front- or rear-facing camera stream
- Add filters, effects, and moderate comments
- Great for casual Q&As, performance, tutorials

2. Voice Chat LIVE

- Go LIVE **without showing your face**
- Only your profile photo is visible, with live audio
- Perfect for podcasts, storytelling, and radio-style sessions

3. Mobile Gaming LIVE

- Stream your **mobile game screen**
- Works for TikTok-integrated games and some supported apps
- Ideal for gamers who want to engage their audience during gameplay

4. TikTok LIVE Studio (Desktop Streaming)

- PC-based streaming software (like OBS or Twitch Studio)
- Connects to your TikTok account via **stream key**
- Advanced options: overlays, split screens, external mics, green screen

5. Using Stream Keys (Pro Setup)

- Access via TikTok LIVE Center (available to approved creators)
- Use for higher production value streams — panels, multi-camera setups, studio-quality audio

The more unique your LIVE experience, the better your chance to grow and retain viewers.

8.3 Planning a Successful LIVE

LIVE isn't just about turning on your camera — it's about showing up with **intention**.

Before You Go LIVE:

- Promote it with a teaser video or story

- Plan a structure (welcome > topic > call-to-action > wrap-up)
- Prepare talking points or props

🎤 During the LIVE:

- Welcome new viewers by name
- Engage with comments — respond out loud
- Pin a message or question to keep the chat focused
- Encourage follows, likes, shares

🎽 End Strong:

- Tease your next LIVE or post
- Thank gifters and top contributors
- Remind people to follow for updates

🛠️ 8.4 LIVE Center Tools & Moderation

TikTok gives creators tools to keep their stream organized and safe.

LIVE Settings Panel Includes:

- **LIVE Gifts toggle**
- **Guest and Multi-Guest options**
- **Comment filters & auto-moderation**
- **Topic selection** (helps TikTok recommend your stream)

Moderation Tools:

- **Block users** or mute for time-based penalties
- Assign a **LIVE Moderator** (trusted follower or team member)
- Set custom **keyword filters** for offensive words or spam

🛡️ *Protect your space — a clean, interactive stream keeps viewers engaged.*

◼️ 8.5 Scheduling & Promoting a LIVE

Use the **LIVE Event tool** to:

- Schedule your LIVE in advance
- Add a countdown to your profile

- Notify your followers when it starts

Combine this with a **teaser video**, Stories, and pinned posts to build anticipation.

◆ 8.6 Monetizing Through LIVE

When you're eligible, you can receive:

- **LIVE Gifts** – Viewers send animated stickers (Diamonds) during your stream
- **LIVE Leads** – Collect emails and info for promotions or business
- **LIVE Subscriptions** – Offer monthly perks like custom badges and subscriber-only chats
- **LIVE Incentive Bonuses** – Based on watch time, streaks, and goals

All earnings go into your **TikTok Balance**, which can be tracked and withdrawn once thresholds are met (more in Chapter 14).

> 💡 *Treat LIVE like a show — the more value you deliver, the more likely viewers will support you financially.*

■ 8.7 LIVE Analytics & Performance

After your stream:

- Visit the **Creator Tools** → **LIVE Center**
- Review:

  - Total views
  - Watch time
  - Followers gained
  - New subscribers
  - Gift count & Diamonds earned

Use this data to refine your next stream's timing, topic, and engagement strategy.

■ Summary: Going LIVE Breakdown

LIVE Type	Best For	Requirements
Standard Camera	Casual Q&As, performances	1,000 followers(depends on location) , age 16+
Voice Chat	Podcasts, chill hangouts	Same as above
Mobile Gaming	Live gameplay	Requires TikTok gaming feature
LIVE Studio (PC)	High-quality or branded streams	Stream key access
Scheduled LIVE	Audience anticipation & growth	Available via LIVE Events tool

TikTok LIVE is where community, monetization, and creativity converge in real time. The more you go LIVE, the better you'll understand your audience — and the more opportunities you'll unlock.

■ 8.8 Setting Up a LIVE Event on TikTok

"If you treat your LIVE like an event, your audience will too."

LIVE Events are TikTok's built-in way to **schedule and promote livestreams** in advance. They create a **shareable event page**, display a countdown on your profile, and send reminders to interested followers. Think of them like virtual flyers for your show.

🔧 How to Create a LIVE Event:

1. **Go to your profile** and tap the **menu (≡)** icon.
2. Select **Creator Tools → LIVE Center**
3. Tap **"Schedule a LIVE"** or **"LIVE Events"** (feature name may vary slightly)
4. Enter your event details:

   ○ **Event title** (max ~32 characters)
   ○ **Start date & time**
   ○ **Duration** (optional)

- ○ **Cover photo** (optional, recommended)

- ○ **Event description** (brief summary of what to expect)

5. Tap **"Create"**

Your LIVE Event will now:

- Show on your profile(bio) with a countdown
- Be visible in your followers' feed as an upcoming event
- Allow users to **"Register"** to receive a notification when you go LIVE .Its FREE

  🗨 **Pro Tip:** Create a teaser video and pin it to your profile. Include a call-to-action: "Tap the countdown to register!"

💡 Event Promotion Tips:

- Use TikTok Stories, pinned videos, and a TikTok LIVE announcement to **build awareness**
- Share your LIVE Event link in DMs, your TikTok bio, and cross-promote on Instagram or YouTube
- Use the **LIVE Event hashtag** to boost visibility (#LiveEvent, #JoinMeLive, etc.)

🎙 8.9 LIVE Etiquette for Guests & Co-Hosts

"A great guest enhances the experience — not hijacks it."

When you're invited to join a **Multi-Guest LIVE**, a **Box Battle**, or **Co-Host session**, you're stepping into a **shared space**. Whether you're appearing casually or as a featured guest, following basic etiquette helps build community and professionalism.

💜 For All Guests:

1. **Be On Time**

   - ○ If it's a scheduled collaboration, show up early and prepared.
   - ○ Delays can disrupt viewer engagement and trust.

2. **Introduce Yourself Briefly**

   - ○ Share your name or handle, your content focus, and a warm greeting.
   - ○ Don't dominate the intro — keep it concise.

3. **Respect the Host's Flow**

- Let the host guide the conversation or set the pace.
- Wait for natural openings before jumping in.

4. **Avoid Over-Self-Promotion**

   - It's okay to share your handle once, but focus on adding value to the stream.
   - Don't spam the comments or direct attention away from the host.

5. **Watch Your Language & Behavior**

   - Follow community guidelines: no bullying, hate speech, explicit content.
   - Hosts can mute or remove you if needed — and TikTok may penalize accounts that misbehave on LIVE.

6. **Engage the Audience**

   - Read and respond to viewer comments.
   - Ask questions or add fun prompts like polls or challenges (if the host approves).

7. **Be Supportive**

   - Compliment others in the chat or guest box.
   - Don't interrupt or correct other guests unless asked to clarify something.

🎭 *Remember: Your goal is to **elevate the stream**, not hijack it.*

🎛 Tech Etiquette Tips:

- Ensure **good lighting and sound** before joining
- Mute your mic if you're in a noisy environment
- Don't join from public spaces with distractions
- Use **headphones** to avoid audio feedback

⬛ What Hosts Should Do for Guests:

- Give a quick intro for each guest when they join
- Let them know the flow ahead of time
- Set the tone early — e.g., "We're keeping things chill and fun today!"
- Use TikTok's moderation tools to remove trolls or control the pace

Whether you're looking to entertain, educate, or just hang out with your followers, there are plenty of creative options to explore. Below are a few types of content that can be live streamed to keep your viewers engaged and coming back for more.

1. Q&A Sessions

Let your followers ask questions in real time. Great for creators, experts, or influencers who want to connect directly with their audience.

2. Behind-the-Scenes

Show what happens off-camera—whether it's how you prepare content, your workspace, or daily life. It builds authenticity and trust with viewers.

3. Product Showcases

Perfect for businesses or creators with merch. Demonstrate how your products work, highlight features, and answer live questions to boost engagement and sales.

4. Tutorials or How-Tos

Teach something—makeup looks, recipes, crafts, workouts, or music lessons. Viewers love to learn live because they can ask questions along the way.

5. Live Performances

Sing, dance, play instruments, or perform stand-up comedy. It's entertaining and shows off your talent to a real-time audience.

6. Gaming Streams

Stream mobile or console games while talking to your viewers. You can share tips, strategies, or just your reactions as you play.

7. Daily Vlogs / "Just Chatting"

Go live while doing everyday activities like cooking, driving, or walking your dog. It's casual, relatable, and invites conversation.

8. Challenges and Dares

Let your audience dare you to do something fun (and safe), or participate in viral TikTok challenges. Interactive and engaging for the audience.

9. Collaborations

Go live with another creator to chat, play games, or debate fun topics. Dual lives are great for cross-promoting to each other's followers.

10. Events and Celebrations

Stream birthdays, launches, holidays, or special moments. People love sharing milestones with creators they follow.

11. Motivational Talks / Advice

Speak about mental health, personal growth, productivity tips, or relationship advice. It can be comforting and inspiring for viewers.

12. Fan Appreciation

Give shoutouts, answer fan questions, or do giveaways. A great way to build a loyal community.

13. ASMR or Relaxation Sessions

Use soothing visuals and sounds to relax your audience. These are surprisingly popular for winding down or sleep support.

14. Fitness or Yoga Sessions

Host live workouts or yoga flows. Viewers can follow along and feel like they're in a real-time class.

15. Live Shopping

Combine entertainment and sales by demoing products viewers can buy directly during the stream. TikTok even supports this natively with their shop feature.

▉ Summary: LIVE Event + Guest Etiquette

Feature	Purpose	Pro Tip
LIVE Event	Schedule and promote livestreams	Add countdown + teaser pinned video
Guest Etiquette	Keep collaboration smooth	Respect the host, avoid self-spam
Co-Host Tools	Multi-guest experience	Plan roles or topics in advance

---

With a properly promoted event and respectful guests, your LIVE can go from a simple broadcast to a **community-driven, content-rich experience** that grows your audience and brand.

Chapter 9: Multi-Guest LIVE, Box Battles & Co-Host Matches

"When LIVE becomes a stage — it's your move, your mic, and your momentum."

As TikTok LIVE evolves, it's no longer just about going live — it's about **hosting an experience**. Whether you're bringing together a panel of creators, facing off in a co-host battle, or organizing a high-stakes box challenge, TikTok now gives you powerful tools to **collaborate, compete, and grow** in real time.

This chapter explores:

- **Multi-Guest LIVE** (now up to 8 participants)

- **Box Battles with real-time eliminations**

- **Co-Host Matches and their strategic power-ups**

👫 9.1 Multi-Guest LIVE (Up to 8 Guests)

Multi-Guest LIVE allows creators to host up to **8 people simultaneously** on a single screen — including the host. Participants are arranged in customizable layouts (grids, lists, or featured speaker view), creating a dynamic virtual space for conversation, competition, and entertainment.

⚫ Best for:

- Panel discussions
- Group games or fan contests
- Talent showcases
- Creator roundtables
- Community hangouts

🛠 How to Start a Multi-Guest LIVE:

1. Tap the **"+" button**, swipe to **LIVE**.
2. Enable **Multi-Guest Mode**.
3. Select a **layout style** (grid, featured view, mic-only).
4. Go LIVE and begin inviting guests by tapping **"Invite"** from your viewer list or from your guest pre-selection.

📷 Host Controls:

- Mute individual or all mics
- Remove or replace guests at any time
- Turn on "apply to join" for viewer participation
- Assign moderators to manage chat or assist
- Appoint a moderator

💡 *Multi-Guest LIVES thrive on structure — plan themes, talking points, and roles to keep the session flowing.*

🥊 9.2 Box Battles (8-Person Elimination Format)

TikTok's **Box Battle** is a high-energy, competitive LIVE format where up to **8 participants** (excluding the host) go head-to-head in real-time gifting rounds. The twist? This isn't a traditional 1v1 — it's an elimination arena.

🔧 How It Works:

- Host starts a **Multi-Guest Box Battle**
- All 8 guests are visible in boxes on screen
- Viewers send **LIVE Gifts** to their favorite guest during each round
- After a **predetermined time limit** (e.g., 2–3 minutes), the **guest with the lowest gift total is eliminated**
- Remaining guests battle again — until 1 winner remains

  🖌 *The intensity ramps up with each round, encouraging more viewer interaction and gifting.*

⚙️ Host Role:

- Moderates the session (host does **not** participate in gifting)
- Calls out eliminations and round transitions
- Can invite new guests from queue if rotation is enabled

⬛ Box Battle Advantages:

- Massive gift-earning potential
- Increases viewer participation through real-time stakes
- Showcases up-and-coming creators to new audiences

  🏆 *It's like TikTok's version of a live talent tournament.*

✖ 9.3 Co-Host Matches & Power-Ups

In a **Co-Host Match**, two creators stream side by side in a timed competition. Viewers send **LIVE Gifts**, and the creator with the highest point total at the end **wins the round**.

But here's what makes it strategic: TikTok includes **Power-Ups** — interactive boosts that change the dynamics mid-match.

🎮 Power-Ups Explained:

Powerup	Function
Boost	Temporarily **doubles** the value of received gifts for a few seconds. Use it to maximize earnings during a gifting rush.
Hammer	Temporarily **blocks** the opponent from receiving gifts for a short duration. Great to use when you're behind.
Gloves	Increases your own gift point multiplier for a short period — more aggressive than Boost, usually with greater effect.
Mist	Blinds the opponent's viewers from seeing the gifting scoreboard temporarily. This causes uncertainty and can slow down their support.
Timer	Extends the match duration slightly, giving your viewers more time to support and catch up.

⏱ *Using power-ups wisely can turn the tide of a losing match — or seal a dominant win.*

🍎 Strategy Tips for Power-Ups:

- Activate **Boost** right after announcing a mini goal (e.g., "Let's hit 10K points in 30 seconds!")

- Use **Hammer** if your opponent is surging ahead
- Save **Gloves** for the final 10 seconds of a close battle

- Deploy **Mist** when you sense the opponent's side is rallying
- Tap **Timer** to buy precious seconds in a tight match

9.4 Best Practices for Group & Competitive LIVE Formats

✔ Host Checklist:

- Set rules, themes, and prize incentives (if any)
- Use pinned comments to guide the audience ("Last round — vote with gifts!")
- Shout out top gifters and participants
- Keep energy high, even between rounds

✔ Guest Tips:

- Have your camera/audio ready before joining
- Thank gifters and acknowledge the host
- Don't spam or over-promote your account
- Be a **good sport** — even when eliminated

💬 *Audiences love respectful competition, not drama. Be memorable for the right reasons.*

Chapter Summary: TikTok's Collaborative LIVE Formats

Feature	Max Participants	Type		Use Case
Multi-Guest LIVE	8 + host	Collaborative		Panels, showcases, themed talks
Box Battle	8 guests	Competitive		Gift-driven elimination tournament
Co-Host Match	2 creators	1v1 Power-Ups	+	Strategic gifting competitions

---

By combining smart collaboration with fun, fast-paced competition, these LIVE formats turn TikTok into a **stage for creativity, community, and content-driven performance**.

Chapter 10: TikTok LIVE Memberships (CREATOR TEAMS)

🔑 What is a TikTok LIVE Membership?

TikTok LIVE Memberships are a feature that allows creators to build exclusive communities and earn support directly from their fans. Think of it like joining a VIP club where fans get special perks, and creators get recurring support through monthly subscriptions.

Unlike one-time gifts, memberships offer creators a more consistent revenue stream while rewarding loyal viewers with access to exclusive features, such as badges, emojis, and even private content.

TikTok LIVE Membership Levels & Popular LIVE Ranking

Joining a LIVE Creator's Team

Joining a creator's team during a TikTok LIVE session is a way for fans to engage more closely with their favorite streamers and become part of a more exclusive, interactive community.

How to Send a "Heart Me" to Join:
To join a creator's team, fans can send a specific virtual gift called the "Heart Me." This gift acts as a request to be added to the team. Once sent, the creator is notified and may accept the viewer into their team. This action not only supports the creator but also opens up access to missions and ranking participation for the fan.

Viewing and Managing Joined Teams:
Users can track the teams they've joined through the LIVE tab or their profile settings. Here, they can view the current level, mission progress, and upcoming milestones. Fans can also leave teams or switch allegiance to another creator, though some platforms might have cooldowns or restrictions.

Membership Missions

TikTok LIVE teams come with daily and weekly missions that encourage ongoing fan engagement.

Sending "Heart Me" Gifts (45 points):
Sending a "Heart Me" gift contributes significantly to the team's mission points—awarding 45 points at a time. This is one of the most impactful ways for team members to support their creators.

Sending Regular Gifts (1 Point per Coin):
Every coin spent on regular gifts during a LIVE session contributes to mission progress. The

more viewers send, the more points a creator and their team accumulate, which helps with ranking and unlocking rewards.

Adding Comments (30 Points):
Engaging through comments during a LIVE session also contributes to missions. Each comment adds 30 points, encouraging team members to be active in chat and foster a vibrant community.

Expiry of Daily Points and How to Claim:
Daily mission points typically reset every 24 hours. Fans should claim any available rewards or progress before the reset to maximize their contributions. Unclaimed points may expire, so it's essential to be active and timely.

Level-Up System

The level-up system rewards fans for their continued participation and engagement with their chosen LIVE creators.

Levels 1–50 Overview:
Fans can progress from level 1 to 50 by participating in missions, sending gifts, and being active during LIVEs. Each level unlocks new perks and is displayed prominently in the team leaderboard.

Rewards per Level:
Each level comes with exclusive rewards such as:

- **Badges** to display next to usernames during LIVE sessions.

- **Celebration Gifts**, such as animations or shoutouts.

- **Entrance Spotlights** that announce your arrival with special effects during a LIVE, signaling VIP status to the creator and other viewers.

Unlocking Exclusive Features:
Higher-level members may unlock private chats, behind-the-scenes content, early access to features, or even direct interactions with the creator. This incentivizes fans to remain engaged and climb the ranks.

Helping Creators Rank in Popular LIVE

Beyond individual recognition, team participation plays a big role in boosting a creator's overall visibility and ranking on TikTok LIVE.

Contributing Points to Creator Standings:
Every action taken by team members—gifting, commenting, and engaging—accumulates

points that contribute to the creator's standing in the Popular LIVE rankings. The more active the team, the better the chances for the creator to be featured or recommended.

Discord Private Channels and Off-Platform Engagement:
Many creators extend their communities to platforms like Discord, where team members can interact, strategize, and stay updated on upcoming LIVEs or events. These channels often include exclusive perks for top-level members, such as AMAs, giveaways, and polls.

Supporting Creators Even When They're Offline:
Team members can continue to support creators by promoting their content, sharing replays, or participating in community challenges. Off-platform loyalty can translate into stronger on-platform performance when the creator goes LIVE again.

Strategic Tips for Fans and Creators

To make the most of the TikTok LIVE membership experience, both fans and creators can adopt strategic habits.

Daily Routines to Level Up:
Fans should aim to complete daily missions like gifting, commenting, and watching LIVEs. Regular participation helps maintain momentum and ensures steady level progression.

Best Practices for Viewers to Stay Active and Visible:

- Join LIVEs early and stay engaged throughout.

- Use unique comments or emojis to stand out.

- Coordinate with other team members to boost visibility and point accumulation during key times.

Creators Optimizing Team Participation:
Creators can boost engagement by:

- Clearly explaining the benefits of joining their team during LIVEs.

- Running mission-focused sessions where fans are encouraged to hit daily goals together.

- Celebrating top team members publicly, fostering a sense of recognition and belonging.

Troubleshooting & Tips

Issue	Possible Fix
"Membership" option not showing	Make sure your account meets all eligibility criteria and has the latest app version
Discord not linking properly	Double-check bot permissions and make sure your invite link isn't expired
Members not renewing	Consider running a short "thank-you" video to re-engage them or offer new perks

In Summary

TikTok LIVE Memberships can transform casual viewers into a tight-knit community of superfans. By giving back with exclusive perks, consistent engagement, and fun missions, you'll unlock new levels of support and content creation freedom.

> "Heart Me" isn't just a button—it's the beginning of a fan journey that helps you grow sustainably as a TikTok creator.

We explore this in details in chapter 12

Chapter 11: Creator League System Explained

The **Creator League** is TikTok LIVE's competitive system that ranks creators based on their **Diamond earnings** over a 30-day period. This system introduces leagues, badges, rewards, and shields to incentivize performance, consistency, and audience engagement. Whether you're new or a veteran LIVE creator, understanding the Creator League can help you climb ranks and gain visibility.

How Does Creator League Ranking Work?

There are **18 total leagues**, grouped into 4 tiers:

- **D League**: D5, D4, D3, D2, D1
- **C League**: C5, C4, C3, C2, C1
- **B League**: B5, B4, B3, B2, B1
- **A League**: A3, A2, A1

Creators start at a tier based on how many **Diamonds** they've collected over the **last 30 days**. Each day, TikTok evaluates creators and updates their league standing. Performance is based on how many Diamonds they earn during LIVE sessions compared to others in their current league.

Fragments and Movement Between Leagues

To move **up** a league, you must collect **4 Fragments**.
To avoid **dropping**, make sure you don't **lose** 4 Fragments.

Here's how Fragment points are earned/lost:

A League (A1 – A3)

Position	Fragment Result
Top 1%	+3 Fragments
Top 1–10%	+2 Fragments
Top 10–20%	+1 Fragment

Bottom 40%   −1 Fragment

B League (B1 – B5)

Position	Fragment Result
Top 1%	+3 Fragments
Top 1–10%	+2 Fragments
Top 10–20%	+1 Fragment
Bottom 40%	−1 Fragment

C League (C1 – C5)

Position	Fragment Result
Top 10%	+2 Fragments
Top 10–20%	+1 Fragment
Bottom 20%	−1 Fragment

D League (D1 – D5)

Position	Fragment Result
Top 10%	+2 Fragments

Top 10–20%   +1 Fragment

Bottom 20%   −1 Fragment

League Shield

To protect creators from sudden drops in rank, TikTok offers a **League Shield**. This activates automatically and prevents the loss of Fragments for a short time.

- **Free to activate**
- Doesn't expire if unused
- You can store up to **10 Shields** at once

Ranking Visibility and Notifications

- You'll see **announcements** at the top of your LIVE when you rise in a League.

- Ranking **notifications** can be toggled on/off:

  - Go to **LIVE > Settings > Ranking**

  Turning this off hides your participation from public leaderboards, but you'll still collect Diamonds and progress privately.

Can You Opt Out of the Creator League?

Yes! Creators can choose not to participate in rankings by:

1. Tapping **Settings > Rankings** on the Go LIVE screen

2. During LIVE, tap **More > Settings > Rankings**

Your data will still be collected and evaluated in the background, but it won't be publicly visible.

Creator League Rewards

If your rankings toggle is **ON**, you are eligible for:

- A **badge** in your League tier (visible to all)
- Exclusive **visual rewards** and bragging rights
- Access to **League-based perks**, such as featured placement in TikTok LIVE's explore tab

---

Eligibility Criteria

To join the Creator League:

- You must host LIVE streams regularly.
- You must **collect Diamonds** during your LIVE sessions.
- You must comply with **TikTok's terms and policies**.

TikTok also **disqualifies** creators who:

- Consistently go LIVE with **inauthentic** or **manipulative** behavior.
- Violate content standards (e.g., promoting trauma, false claims, excessive gift solicitation).
- Frequently use **group LIVE events** (with 3+ creators in a coordinated broadcast more than 2x per 30 days).

! If you believe you've been wrongly excluded, you can file an appeal using the **"Report a Problem"** feature in the app.

Chapter 12: Understanding the Gifter Level-Up Program

TikTok's dynamic ecosystem thrives on interaction and appreciation, especially within the LIVE feature. The **Gifter Level-Up Program** is TikTok's way of recognizing and rewarding those viewers who consistently support their favorite creators by sending virtual gifts. This program transforms passive viewing into an engaging and rewarding experience, where generosity doesn't go unnoticed.

Whether you're new to TikTok LIVE or an experienced supporter, understanding how the Gifter Level-Up Program works will allow you to maximize your visibility, unlock unique perks, and enjoy a deeper connection with creators.

What Is the Gifter Level-Up Program?

The Gifter Level-Up Program is a **tiered experience-based system** that allows viewers to **accumulate experience points (XP)** by sending gifts during LIVE broadcasts. The more you gift, the higher your gifter level grows. Your gifter level becomes a **visible status symbol**, reflecting your engagement, loyalty, and presence across TikTok LIVE.

This isn't just for show — it opens up a variety of **interactive effects, exclusive gifts**, and **social privileges**.

> 👕 **You gain 1 experience point for every 1 Coin used on gifts during a LIVE video.**

Note: Gifts sent in short-form videos, posts, or outside LIVE sessions **do not count** toward your Gifter Level. Only LIVE gifting contributes to the program.

The Benefits of Leveling Up

Leveling up unlocks a wide range of perks designed to **highlight your support** and **enhance your experience**. The higher your level, the more impressive and visible your participation becomes.

These rewards may include:

- Custom **gifter badges** that evolve visually as you level up
- **Celebration effects** that play when you enter a LIVE or level up
- Access to **high-tier exclusive gifts**, some costing tens of thousands of Coins
- Priority **visibility in chats** and **recognition from creators**

It's a built-in way to be **seen, celebrated, and appreciated**.

Gifter Levels and Rewards: Tier Breakdown

Level	Rewards & Unlocks
Lv.1	Initial badge – ▐ shows basic supporter status
Lv.5	Unlock small celebratory visual gifts (e.g. cakes, stickers)
Lv.10	Badge II – enhanced appearance + unlock mid-tier gifts
Lv.20	Badge III – "Thank you" animations, themed effects
Lv.30	Badge IV – Access to creator greeting animations, entrance flair
Lv.40	Badge V – Animated entrances, unlock elite gifts (e.g. 🧸, 🌠)
Lv.50 +	Badge VI – Full celebration package: wings, phoenix gifts, and more

Exclusive gifts available to Lv.40+ gifters can cost **34,999 to 42,999 Coins**, such as:

- **Mythical Pegasus**
- **Fiery Phoenix**
- **Crystal Icebird**
- TikTok-themed luxury gifts

Tracking Progress and Viewing Rewards

To view your Gifter Level and see how close you are to your next badge or reward:

1. Tap the **[Gift]** icon in any LIVE video

2. Look for the **progress bar** at the bottom of the gifting panel

3. Tap the bar to open your **Gifter Dashboard**, where you can see:

   - Current level and XP progress

   - Rewards you've unlocked

   - Gifts you're eligible to send

   - How many more Coins you need to level up

This system provides transparency, motivation, and a goal-oriented experience as you support your favorite creators.

Freezing and Reactivating Your Gifter Level

Your Gifter Level status remains active **as long as you engage regularly**. However, if you stop gifting for a period of time, TikTok pauses your activity in the program.

What triggers a freeze:

- You do not send any LIVE gifts for **7 consecutive days**

- The countdown starts **only on days when your favorite creators go LIVE**

What happens when frozen:

- Your **gifter badge and rewards become inactive**

- Entrance animations and other visual perks are temporarily removed

- You'll receive **notifications on day 5 and 6** to warn you before freezing

How to reactivate:

- Simply send **1 gift (any value)** during a LIVE session to resume your gifter status and re-enable rewards

Your XP and level **remain intact** unless you delete your account.

How to Opt Out (and Back In)

Some users may prefer not to participate in the Gifter Level-Up Program, especially if they want to support creators more discreetly. TikTok offers full flexibility to **pause or opt out** of the program at any time.

Steps to Opt Out:

1. Go to **[Settings] > Gifter Level-Up Program**

2. Tap **"Turn Off"**

When opted out:

- You'll stop earning XP
- Your badge and privileges will be hidden
- You will no longer appear in celebration animations

To rejoin:

- Simply turn the program **back ON**
- Your progress will be restored to where you left off
- If your account was deleted in the meantime, progress cannot be recovered

---

Why Participate in the Gifter Program?

Here's why many users aim to climb the Gifter Ladder:

- **Stand out in chat:** Your badge and level help you stand out during high-traffic LIVEs
- **Earn creator appreciation:** Creators often give special recognition to top gifters
- **Gain access to rare gifts:** Only unlocked through consistent support
- **Build reputation:** Be seen as a dedicated community member, not just a viewer
- **Get noticed faster:** Higher-tier gifters often enjoy more interactions from creators

🎤 *"It's not just about Coins—it's about community. When a top gifter enters, we notice." – TikTok LIVE Creator*

Tips for Efficient Gifting

- Focus on creators you follow or frequent—this helps build recognition
- Time your gifting during creator events or **bonus moments** to maximize impact
- Mix large and small gifts to maintain engagement across days
- Join in **LIVE gifting battles** where support has extra visibility

Final Thoughts

The Gifter Level-Up Program enhances TikTok LIVE by turning appreciation into **tangible status, visual flair, and exclusive access**. Whether you're giving small gifts to many or focusing your energy on supporting a favorite creator, this program adds an exciting layer of interaction to the LIVE experience. You don't just watch — you participate. And the more you do, the more TikTok rewards you.

Ready to learn how you can earn **real-world rewards** from TikTok too?

Chapter 13: Monetization & Creator Programs

"Your creativity has value — and TikTok has built the tools to help you cash in."

TikTok isn't just a platform for trends and entertainment. It has evolved into a full-fledged **income ecosystem** for creators, entrepreneurs, streamers, and even casual users. Whether you're going LIVE, uploading short-form videos, promoting products, or offering exclusive content, TikTok provides multiple paths to **monetize your content, audience, and influence**.

This chapter breaks down every major monetization tool available to users, how to access them, the eligibility requirements, how payouts work, and how to combine programs for maximum earning potential.

🏛 13.1 Overview of TikTok's Monetization Paths

TikTok offers monetization through a mix of **platform-run programs** and **user-driven opportunities**. These include:

A. Direct Monetization by TikTok:

- Creator Rewards Program (formerly Creator Fund)
- LIVE Gifts & LIVE Match Battles
- Subscriptions
- LIVE Incentive Program
- Gaming Creator Program
  Video Reward Bonuses (TikTok Studio)

B. Commerce Monetization:

- TikTok Shop (For Creators)

- TikTok Shop (For Sellers)

- Affiliate Commissions

C. Sponsored Collaborations:

- Work With Artists

- Brand partnerships

- Creator Marketplace (via Creator Center)

Let's break each one down.

🧠 13.2 Creator Rewards Program

This is TikTok's **video performance-based reward system**, replacing the Creator Fund in many regions. As of April 15, 2025, the TikTok Creator Rewards Program is available to creators who are located in the following countries:

- **United States**
- **United Kingdom**
- **France**
- **Germany**
- **Japan**
- **South Korea**
- **Brazil**

It's important to note that TikTok may expand this list in the future, so creators in other regions should keep an eye out for updates.

📌 Eligibility:

- Be 18+ years old
- Have **10,000+ followers**
- At least **100,000 video views in the last 30 days**
  Use a **public Creator or Business account**
- Follow TikTok's **Community Guidelines**

🎬 How It Works:

- Eligible creators earn money based on **video engagement** (views, watch time, interactions).
- Income is distributed **monthly**.
- View stats and estimated earnings via **Creator Tools > Creator Rewards Program**.

  🔍 *Higher retention + niche content = better payouts.*

  Keep in mind that meeting these criteria doesn't guarantee entry into the program, and TikTok has the final say on eligibility. If you reside in one of the listed countries and meet the requirements, you can typically apply for the program through the TikTok app in your "Creator Tools" section.

🎁 13.3 LIVE Gifts & Subscriptions

TikTok defines "Live Gifts" as **virtual items that viewers can send to creators during a TikTok LIVE video as a way to show their appreciation and support in real-time.**

Here's a more detailed breakdown of what that means:

- **Virtual Tokens of Appreciation:** Live Gifts are essentially digital tokens that viewers purchase using TikTok Coins (TikTok's in-app currency). These coins are bought with real money.
- **Displayed as Animations:** When a viewer sends a Live Gift, it appears on the live stream as an animated sticker or icon. This provides a visual way for the creator to see the support and for other viewers to witness the interaction.
- **Variety of Gifts with Different Values:** There's a range of Live Gifts available, each with a different coin value. These can range from simple and inexpensive gifts like a "Rose" to more elaborate and costly ones like a "TikTok Universe."
- **Converted to Diamonds for Creators:** Creators who receive Live Gifts accumulate "Diamonds" based on the value of the gifts they get. TikTok then allows creators to convert these Diamonds into real money, although TikTok takes a percentage as a fee. The general estimate is that one Diamond is worth roughly half the value of one Coin.
- **Interactive Element:** Sending Live Gifts is a way for viewers to stand out in the live chat and get the creator's attention. Many creators will acknowledge gifters with shout-outs or other forms of recognition.
- **Monetization Tool for Creators:** Live Gifts provide a direct way for TikTok creators to monetize their live content and earn income based on the support of their audience.

In simpler terms: Imagine you're watching your favorite creator's live stream, and you're really enjoying it. TikTok Live Gifts allow you to send them a little "virtual applause" in the form of a digital sticker that costs you some TikTok Coins. The creator then receives the value of that gift (minus TikTok's cut) as Diamonds, which they can eventually turn into cash. It's a way for fans to directly support the creators they love.

● LIVE Gifts

- Viewers send virtual gifts during your livestream.
- These convert into **Diamonds**, which are then converted into real money.
- You can withdraw earnings through PayPal or linked bank accounts.

    ● *1 Diamond ≈ $0.005 USD (subject to region and tax).*

Requirements:

- 1,000+ followers
  Age 18+
- Go LIVE regularly and follow TikTok's content policies

    ◆ LIVE Subscription Program

This allows creators to offer **monthly subscriptions** to followers in exchange for perks:

- Custom emojis
- Subscriber-only chat
- Loyalty badges
- Exclusive LIVEs or Q&As

Requirements:

- Be invited or apply via **Creator Center**
- Age 18+, compliant with TikTok's policies
- Stream consistently

🎮 13.4 LIVE Incentive Program

A hidden gem for regular LIVE streamers.

TikTok rewards creators with **bonus Diamonds** when they reach **LIVE goals**, such as:

- Going LIVE for **a certain number of minutes**
- Hosting for **multiple consecutive days**
  Reaching engagement milestones (viewers, comments)

💡 *Bonus incentives often change monthly — check "LIVE Center > LIVE Task" regularly.*

🎮 13.5 Gaming Creator Program

If you stream mobile or desktop games via TikTok LIVE or LIVE Studio, you can qualify for **Gaming monetization**, which includes:

- **Game-specific bonuses** (e.g. for streaming Genshin Impact, PUBG, etc.)
- **Priority placement in the Gaming tab**
- Sponsored gift events or bounty board missions

  💬 *Use TikTok LIVE Studio (desktop) for the best streaming experience.*

🔒 13.6 TikTok Shop for Creators

TikTok's native e-commerce platform allows creators to:

- Sell physical/digital products
- Promote others' products as an affiliate
- Host **LIVE Shopping streams** and earn per sale

Creator Benefits:

- Earn **commissions** (up to 20–50%) by linking products in videos/LIVEs
- Run **flash sales**, **product demos**, and **tutorials**
- View orders and sales via **TikTok Shop Dashboard**

Requirements:

- 1,000+ followers (in most regions)
- Consistent content posting
- ID verification

🛒 13.7 TikTok Shop for Sellers

If you run a business, you can also sign up as a **TikTok Shop Seller**:

- List your own products (inventory or dropshipping)
- Integrate with Shopify or WooCommerce
- Offer affiliate commission to creators who promote your products

Great for:

- Clothing brands, beauty products, gadgets, niche stores
- Creators who want to **transition into eCommerce**

🎧 13.8 Work With Artists (Music & Sound Collabs)

This feature connects creators with musicians looking to **promote their songs**. You get paid to:

- Use specific tracks in your videos
- Participate in hashtag challenges
- Help songs go viral on TikTok

🎧 *Your creativity = music's success. This is how artists launch hits.*

📣 13.9 Brand Partnerships & Creator Marketplace

The **Creator Marketplace** is TikTok's official hub where:

- Brands browse, vet, and hire creators for sponsored posts

- Creators showcase their niche, pricing, audience stats

Requirements:

- 10K+ followers
- Consistent engagement
- Verified ID and public profile

Payouts vary based on:

- Audience size
- Location
- Niche (finance & beauty pay more than comedy, for example)

💰 13.10 Cashing Out: TikTok Earnings

All eligible monetization earnings go into your **TikTok Balance**, visible via:

- **Settings > Balance**
- Or via **Creator Tools > Earnings**

Minimum withdrawal amount:

- **$10–$100**, depending on the program and region

Methods:

- **PayPal**
- **Bank Transfer**
- **Transfer to TikTok Wallet**

  ⚠️ TikTok may withhold a percentage for **regional tax** and **service fees**. Always read payout terms.

◼ 13.11 Maximizing Your Monetization Strategy

To earn consistently on TikTok, consider the **3-Layer Monetization Model**:

Layer	Tools to Use	Goal

Content Layer	Creator Rewards, Work With Artists	Earn from what you post
Community Layer	LIVE Gifts, Subscriptions, Creator Teams	Earn from loyal fans
Commerce Layer	TikTok Shop, Affiliate links	Earn by selling or promoting

Bonus Tip: Bundle these tools!
→ Host a LIVE shopping event → use trending audio (Work With Artists) → include TikTok Shop links → collect gifts AND commissions.

🎞 13.12 Common Disqualifiers and Pitfalls

You can be banned or disqualified from monetization if you:

- Violate community or LIVE guidelines (even once)
- Use misleading titles or gift-begging phrases
- Participate in mass engagement "loops" or "drops"
- Share banned or sensitive content (fake giveaways, financial scams, etc.)

TikTok takes monetization violations seriously and can permanently disable features or remove earnings.

■ 13.13 Tools to Monitor Monetization

- **Creator Center** (for analytics and insights)
- **LIVE Center** (for stream goals and tasks)
- **Studio.TikTok.com** (advanced dashboard for pro creators)
- **Affiliate Portal** (track product commissions & top sellers)

💬 Use your data. If a video earns more than others — analyze why. Then double down.

⬤ Final Takeaway

Monetization on TikTok is no longer a bonus — it's an **intentional system** that rewards creativity, consistency, and community-building.

You don't need millions of followers. You need to:

- Know your audience
- Use the right tools
  Deliver content with value

How to Buy TikTok Coins

You can buy Coins within the TikTok app using third-party platforms like the Apple App Store or Google Play Store. In regions where it's supported, you also have the option to purchase them directly on the TikTok website at www.tiktok.com/coin. In some locations, Coins might be available as gift cards that you can redeem on the TikTok site.

Important: You need to be at least 18 years old (or 19 in South Korea) to buy Coins. The purchase and use of Coins must comply with our Virtual Items Policy.

To Add Coins to Your TikTok Account:

Using Your Account Balance:

1. Open the TikTok app and tap on your Profile at the bottom.
2. Go to Settings and privacy, then tap on Balance.
3. Select "Get Coins" or tap your current balance to choose a Coins package to purchase.
4. Complete the purchase by following the instructions provided via your app store.

During a LIVE Session:

1. While watching a LIVE video in the TikTok app, tap the Gift icon at the bottom. (If you don't see the Gifts option, gifting isn't enabled for that LIVE session.)
2. Tap on "Recharge" or the Coin icon, then choose your preferred Coins package.
3. Follow the prompts to finish the purchase through your app store.

From a TikTok Post:

1. In the TikTok app, select the Comments button on the post.
2. Tap the Gifts icon in the comment section. (If the Gifts icon is absent, gifting is not available on that post.)
3. Tap on "Recharge" or the Coin icon and select the Coins package you want.
4. Complete the purchase as directed through your app store.

Using the TikTok Website (Provides best cash for coins value):

1. Visit www.tiktok.com/coin.
2. Pick the Coins package you wish to buy.
3. Click on "Recharge."
4. Follow the instructions to complete the payment using your chosen payment method.

Payment Methods 👍

Major credit or debit cards (for example, Visa, MasterCard, etc.)

PayPal, in regions where this option is supported.

Based on the many sources that have been indexed, TikTok offers numerous payment methods for buying coins, and the exact options can vary based on your country or region, billing settings, and the platform you're using (app vs. website). To provide examples of local payment methods that users might see depending on their country, here are some specific examples:

- **Asia Pacific (APAC):**
  - In Indonesia, you might see local digital wallets and online bank transfers such as **Dana, OVO, ShopeePay, or GoPay.**
  - In the Philippines, you may have options including **Maya** or **GCash** along with standard bankcards and PayPal.
- **Europe, Middle East, and Africa (EMEA):**
  - Users in some European countries might see regional options like **Klarna,PIONEER , AT EPS,** or **SEPA Direct Debit** alongside traditional credit and debit cards.
  - In countries like Egypt, you could see methods such as **Fawry** (a local payment system).
- **North America:**
  - The prevalent methods are typically **credit/debit cards, PayPal, Apple Pay, and Google Pay.**

These examples are not exhaustive but illustrate how TikTok tailors its payment options to local markets to better accommodate different currencies, banking systems, and local digital wallet providers. If you're looking to see which exact methods are available in your country, it's best to check the payment section when you make a purchase on TikTok or consult the help sections provided by TikTok's business support resources.

TikTok Scaled LIVE Rewards – Easy Guide

If you're a TikTok creator who goes LIVE, TikTok now offers **extra rewards** based on how active and engaging your LIVE videos are. Here's a step-by-step guide to help you understand how it all works and how to **earn up to 53%** in rewards.

---

1. What Are Scaled LIVE Rewards?

This is TikTok's way of rewarding creators for doing quality LIVE streams. The more you go LIVE and keep your viewers engaged, the higher your reward percentage.

You can earn:

- **Up to 40%** from each LIVE (Per-LIVE Missions)
- **Up to 13%** extra from Weekly Missions
  = Up to 53% in total

---

2. How to Earn Rewards

A. Per-LIVE Missions (Up to 40%)

These are calculated right after each LIVE ends.

Activity	Rewards %
Go LIVE for 25+ mins	38%
Gain 5+ new followers	2%
Go LIVE 10 mins+	35%

Lower durations give you smaller %

Tip: Longer LIVE sessions and more followers = more rewards!

B. Weekly Missions (Up to 13%)

Calculated based on your full week's performance and added every **Monday**.

Ways to earn:

- **Go LIVE Days** (25+ mins per day):
    - 1 day = 6%
    - 2+ days = 8%
- **Content Engagement (from your team/fans):**

- 10+ active members = 1%

- 100+ = 1.5%

- 2000+ = 2%

- **Creator League** (up to 3%):

  - Level up your league = 3%
  - Stay in your current A1–A3 League = 1%

3. What Are Diamonds?

Diamonds are TikTok's way of measuring how popular your LIVE is. Viewers send you **Gifts** or **Star Comments**, which turn into Diamonds.

More Diamonds = More reward money!

Example:

- 10,000 Diamonds with a 51% reward rate = **$51**

4. When Do I Get Paid?

- **Per-LIVE rewards:** Added after each LIVE ends.
- **Weekly rewards:** Added every Monday based on your past week's results.

5. How to Check Your Rewards

Go to:

LIVE Rewards > Weekly Statements

6. Avoiding Penalties (Content Quality Adjustments)

TikTok may reduce your rewards if:

- You break **Community** or **Monetization Guidelines**
- You violate LIVE rules

Good to know:

- Penalties are reviewed by humans, not AI
- You can **appeal** any deduction (within 180 days)

7. How to Appeal a Deduction

Go to:

> Transaction Details > Find the LIVE video
> Submit your appeal. Most are reviewed in **under 30 minutes**. If approved, TikTok gives your rewards back.

TikTok's **Effect Creator Rewards** program

TikTok's **Effect Creator Rewards** program lets creators earn cash for popular AR effects built in Effect House. Eligible creators (18+ in supported regions, with a Gold/Platinum/Diamond badge, at least five published effects and 3 effects used in 1,000 qualified videos each) can apply and track rewards in the desktop Rewards Center Effect House. Effects must be created in the Effect House desktop tool and hit 5,000 unique public video publishes within 30 days to qualify; rewards start accruing at 100,000 publishes, with a maximum payout of $14,000 per effect and $50,000 per creator per month, paid out monthly once earnings exceed $10 USD

Official TikTok Monetization Options for U.S. Creators ONLY(2025)

In the United States, TikTok offers a variety of official monetization programs that allow creators to earn money directly through the platform. Below is a detailed overview of each program, how they work, their eligibility requirements, and any notable recent updates:

TikTok Creator Fund (2020–2023)

The TikTok Creator Fund, launched in 2020, was a program where creators earned money based on their video views and engagement. Creators needed to be at least 18 years old, have over 10,000 followers, and accumulate 100,000 video views in the past 30 days to qualify. The fund, which initially had over $1 billion allocated for creators over three years, received criticism due to low payouts.

Update: In 2023, TikTok phased out the Creator Fund, replacing it with a new rewards program that promises higher earning potential.

TikTok Creator Rewards Program (Creativity Program Beta)

Introduced in early 2023 as an upgrade to the Creator Fund, the TikTok Creator Rewards Program (formerly the Creativity Program Beta) focuses on rewarding creators for high-quality, original videos, particularly those longer than one minute. Creators can earn significantly higher payouts compared to the old fund, with TikTok noting the potential for up to 20x the rewards. To qualify, creators must be 18+, have at least 10,000 followers, and 100,000 valid video views in the last 30 days, while also adhering to TikTok's content guidelines.

This program is now the primary method for TikTok to share video-view revenue with creators.

TikTok Pulse (Ad Revenue Sharing)

TikTok Pulse is an ad revenue-sharing program where top creators earn a share of ad earnings. It places brand ads alongside the top 4% of trending videos, and creators whose videos are featured in this program receive 50% of the ad revenue.

Eligibility: Currently, only U.S. creators with at least 100,000 followers are eligible for Pulse, and they must adhere to community guidelines and post consistently.

Update: Launched in mid-2022, Pulse is an exclusive program, primarily for creators with significant reach.

TikTok Series (Paid Premium Content)

Launched in 2023, TikTok Series allows creators to monetize premium content by placing it behind a paywall. Each Series can include up to 80 videos (each up to 20 minutes long), and viewers pay a one-time fee to access the collection. This feature offers a new way for creators to directly monetize long-form, exclusive content on TikTok.

Eligibility: Creators must be 18+, have an account older than 30 days, and meet a few content-based requirements (e.g., having at least 10,000 followers and 1,000 views in the last 30 days). Creators with slightly fewer than 10,000 followers may still apply if they have sold premium content elsewhere.

TikTok Creator Marketplace

The TikTok Creator Marketplace is the platform's official tool for brand collaborations, allowing creators to connect with brands for sponsored deals and paid campaigns. Brands can discover and reach out to creators, and creators can browse available campaigns to join.

Eligibility: Creators must be 18+ with a substantial following (TikTok now allows creators with around 10,000 followers to join in the U.S.), and their account must be in good standing.

TikTok Shop & Affiliate Program

TikTok Shop allows creators to earn money by tagging products in their videos or live streams, either by selling their own products or earning affiliate commissions on items sold by others.

Eligibility (U.S.): Creators must be 18+ and have about 5,000 followers to apply for the TikTok Shop Affiliate Program. Accounts must be in good standing.

Update: TikTok Shop became widely available in the U.S. in 2023, providing a new revenue stream through social commerce.

TikTok LIVE Gifts (Virtual Gifting on Live Streams)

Viewers can send virtual gifts during live streams, which creators can convert into real money. The amount of gifts depends on the stream's popularity and engagement.

Eligibility: To receive LIVE Gifts, creators must be 18+, have at least 1,000 followers (to unlock the ability to go live), and be in a region where gifting is available.

TikTok Video Gifts (Gifts on Non-Live Videos)

Similar to LIVE Gifts, Video Gifts allow viewers to send virtual gifts to creators on regular TikTok videos. Creators receive Diamonds, which they can redeem for real money based on video engagement.

Eligibility: Creators must be at least 18 years old, have 10,000 followers, and meet TikTok's safety moderation standards.

TikTok Tips (Direct Monetary Tips)

TikTok Tips is a feature that enables viewers to send direct tips to creators as a one-time donation. Unlike virtual gifts, Tips are actual money (processed through Stripe), and creators receive 100% of the tip value.

Eligibility (U.S.): Creators need to be 18+ and have around 100,000 followers to access the Tips feature.

Update: The Tips feature rolled out widely in late 2021, offering creators a way for fans to provide direct financial support.

TikTok LIVE Subscription (Subscriber Badges & Exclusive Content)

This feature allows creators to earn recurring revenue by offering a subscription service. Fans can subscribe to a creator's live streams for a monthly fee, receiving perks like exclusive content, badges, and custom emotes.

Eligibility: To access the full subscription feature (including multi-tier plans), creators need at least 10,000 followers and 100,000 video views in the last 30 days. Smaller creators with 1,000 followers can access basic live subscriptions.

Update: In late 2024, TikTok expanded this feature to allow creators to offer exclusive content outside of live streams.

TikTok Effect Creator Rewards

TikTok launched this program in May 2023 to reward creators who design AR effects and filters using TikTok's Effect House platform. Creators can earn money based on user engagement with their effects.

Eligibility: Creators must be 18+ and use the Effect House platform to build effects. Payouts depend on how widely the effect is used.

TikTok Branded Missions

Branded Missions is an ad collaboration feature where creators can submit videos to participate in campaigns for brands. If a brand selects a creator's video, they receive a payment and their video gets promoted.

Eligibility: Creators must be 18+ and have over 1,000 followers to participate in Branded Missions.

Update: In 2023, TikTok expanded this feature to more regions and brands, offering an additional monetization opportunity for creators.

Each of the above options is an official TikTok program, allowing creators to monetize their content directly through the platform. Creators can mix and match these options (e.g., earning through the Creator Rewards Program while receiving LIVE Gifts).

It's important to note that all programs require compliance with TikTok's Community Guidelines, and TikTok frequently updates eligibility and features to expand opportunities for creators. This list reflects the current monetization tools available in 2025, excluding external methods (like off-platform brand deals or affiliate links).

By leveraging these built-in programs, U.S. TikTok creators can generate income through views, fan support, brand partnerships, and more—all within the TikTok ecosystem.

Sources: TikTok's official announcements and help center, along with recent news updates.

Chapter 14: TikTok Studio – Dashboard, Analytics & Bonus Tools

"Data is your compass. Studio is your map."

TikTok Studio is more than just a backend tool — it's the **central nervous system** of your content journey. Whether you're aiming to grow, monetize, analyze, or collaborate, Studio is where you track your evolution and make informed decisions as a content creator, business owner, or influencer.

This chapter will give you:

- A **full walkthrough** of each section of TikTok Studio
- Breakdown of **critical metrics** and how to interpret them
- Tools to **optimize your performance and income**
  Advanced tips to use Studio like a **professional creator**

● 14.1 What Is TikTok Studio (And Who Is It For)?

TikTok Studio is TikTok's official content management platform for:

- **Video creators**
- **LIVE streamers**
- **Shop sellers**
- **Affiliate marketers**
- **Brand collaborators**

Studio is designed to centralize:

- Your **content**
- Your **analytics**
- Your **monetization**
- Your **campaigns and collaborations**

📌 It works as a **web dashboard** (studio.tiktok.com) or can be accessed from within the **TikTok mobile app** via Creator Tools.

→▮ 14.2 How to Access TikTok Studio

On Mobile:

- Open TikTok → Profile → ☰ Menu → **Creator Tools** → **TikTok Studio**

On Desktop:

- Go to studio.tiktok.com and log in

💡 The desktop version has advanced filtering, longer analytics time frames, and better display for side-by-side comparisons.

🖥️ 14.3 TikTok Studio Layout Breakdown

Studio is organized into tabs that reflect your **entire creator lifecycle**:

⬛ A. Dashboard Overview

A summary panel showing your most important metrics in one place.

Metrics Include:

- Total video views
- Engagement rate (likes, shares, comments)
- Follower change
- Watch time trends
- Estimated revenue (from Rewards, LIVE, Shop)

Use this section to:

- Get a quick health check of your content
- See what needs attention (drop in views? slow follower growth?)

⬛ *Think of this as your daily performance snapshot.*

🎥 B. Content Management

This section is your **content library and editor**.

Features include:

- Upload new videos (on desktop)
- See all your past posts
- Draft manager
- Edit titles, captions, hashtags

- Add TikTok Shop links to existing videos
- Check copyright status (muted sounds, flagged content)

🛠 *Use filters to quickly find your most-viewed, most-saved, or highest-converting videos.*

🔍 C. Analytics: Deep-Dive Performance Tracking

Breakdown by Video:

- Views (hour-by-hour & daily)
- Average watch time
- Audience retention graph
- Sources of traffic (FYP, Following, Search, Profile)
- Audience location, gender, and active hours

Breakdown by Account:

- Follower growth over time
- Net gain/loss
- Content-type breakdown (e.g., LIVE vs. posts)
- Audience interests

📓 *Use the retention graph to find where people drop off in your videos — then rewrite your intros or improve pacing.*

⚫ D. LIVE Center

Everything about your LIVE performance is tracked here.

Includes:

- Total LIVE sessions
- Peak concurrent viewers
- Diamonds earned (gift breakdown)
- Average watch time per LIVE
- Most engaged viewers & top gifters
- Scheduled upcoming LIVEs

Bonus Tools:

- Set reminders or auto-publish LIVE events

- Apply for LIVE programs (e.g., subscription beta)

- Access **LIVE Task Center** (for bonus payouts)

Use the "viewer loyalty" chart to identify potential moderators or superfans.

E. Earnings Tab

Tracks all sources of revenue from TikTok:

Earnings Type	Source
Creator Rewards	From video performance (watch time, engagement)
LIVE Gifts	From Diamonds earned during livestreams
LIVE Subscriptions	Monthly recurring revenue from fans
TikTok Shop	Commissions from affiliate or personal products
Sponsored Campaigns	Brand deal payouts via Creator Marketplace
Missions & Bonuses	Payouts for streaks, challenges, and TikTok-run events

Payout Tools:

- Connect PayPal or bank account
- Set payout schedule (weekly/monthly)
- View withdrawal history

■ *Minimum withdrawal amount is typically $10–$100 USD depending on region and program.*

■ F. Tools & Utilities

Creator Tools:

- Basic video editing (cut, trim, subtitles)
- Cover image selection
- Caption generation + trending hashtags
- Upload tool (drag & drop or mobile sync)

Monetization Settings:

- Enable/disable Creator Rewards
- Opt in/out of rankings or gifting
- Set live schedules and banner promotions
- Monitor violation status (LIVE suspensions, copyright, etc.)

● 14.4 Bonus Center & Tasks (The "Side Quests" of TikTok)

This is where you'll find **missions** — time-limited activities TikTok offers creators to increase content output and engagement.

Examples:

- Post 3 videos in 5 days

- Go LIVE for 1 hour/day for 3 consecutive days

- Use a trending sound and reach 5k views

Rewards include:

- Cash bonuses

- Featured content placement

- Exclusive filters, badges, or celebration animations

- Early access to monetization tools

🧠 Check the Bonus Center weekly — missions rotate and often align with holidays or marketing events.

✏️ 14.5 Advanced Data Interpretation: What To Watch For

Metric	What It Tells You	What To Do With It
Average Watch Time	Content retention quality	Improve your hook/intro or shorten your video
Top Traffic Source	Best-performing discovery channel	Double down on trending hashtags or SEO titles
Completion Rate	If viewers stay to the end	Identify ideal video length
Gift Distribution (LIVE)	Viewer loyalty & gifting cycles	Engage more with top gifters, create team incentives
Posting Time Effectiveness	Which hours drive engagement	Schedule content during peak windows

---

🚀 14.6 Pro Tips for Using Studio Like a Full-Time Creator

1. **Download analytics reports weekly** for content planning

2. **Test new formats** (e.g., a series) and use Studio to compare results

3. **Tag collaborators and products** using Studio's link tool

4. **Watch your RPM (Revenue per Mille)** if you're in the Rewards Program

5. **Benchmark your growth every 30 days** using the custom date filter

---

█ Summary: TikTok Studio = Creator Clarity

Tool	Use Case
Dashboard	Overall content & growth snapshot
Content Manager	Upload, edit, organize videos
Analytics	Understand what's working (and why)
LIVE Center	Track LIVE income, engagement & growth
Bonus Center	Join missions, earn rewards
Earnings Tab	Monitor revenue streams & payouts
Studio Access Web	Use full-screen tools for pro planning

By learning to use TikTok Studio not just as a stats viewer — but as a **strategic compass** — you'll build more than just content.

You'll build a creative career, brand presence, and revenue stream grounded in **data-driven decisions**.

Chapter 15: TikTok LIVE Cash-Out Process & Withdrawal Tips

"You've earned it. Now let's cash it out."

So you've been going LIVE, collecting gifts, earning Diamonds, and participating in monetization programs — but **how do you actually get paid**?

TikTok offers several ways for creators to **withdraw their earnings**, whether it's from LIVE Gifts, the Creator Rewards Program, or TikTok Shop sales. While the system is designed to be simple, it helps to understand all the steps, options, and best practices to make the most of your payouts.

This chapter will walk you through:

- Understanding how TikTok rewards convert to real money
- Withdrawal limits and methods
- Setting up your payment information
- Common cash-out issues and how to resolve them
- Pro tips for smooth and regular withdrawals

◆ 15.1 Understanding Diamonds and Coin Conversion

👕 TikTok's Gifting Currency System:

- **Viewers** purchase Coins using real money (e.g., 100 Coins = ~$1.29 USD).
- Coins are used to send **virtual gifts** (e.g., Roses, Lions, Rockets) during LIVE sessions. Creators receive those gifts as **Diamonds**.

- **Diamonds can be converted into real money.**

  💰 **1 Diamond ≈ $0.005 USD**
  (This value can fluctuate slightly by region and currency exchange.)

📇 Example:

- You receive 20,000 Coins in gifts during one LIVE.
- TikTok converts those to approximately 10,000 Diamonds.
- That's roughly **$50 USD** in withdrawable funds.

📁 15.2 How to Check Your TikTok Balance

To view your earnings:

1. Open TikTok and go to your **Profile**
2. Tap the **☰ Menu > Settings and privacy**
3. Scroll to **Balance**
4. Here you'll see:

   - **Recharge Balance** (your own Coins)
   - **LIVE Gifts / Diamonds**
   - **TikTok Shop earnings** (if applicable)
   - **Withdrawable balance**

You can tap **"LIVE Gifts"** to see Diamonds collected, conversion rates, and withdrawal history.

🏛 15.3 How to Withdraw Your Earnings

To cash out your Diamonds:

1. Go to **Settings > Balance > LIVE Gifts**
2. Tap **"Withdraw"**
3. Select your preferred **payment method**:

   - **PayPal** (most common)
   - **Bank transfer** (available in select regions)
4. Enter your details and **verify your identity**
5. Choose withdrawal amount and confirm

   ■ Withdrawals typically take **3–5 business days** to process. During high volume, it may take up to 10 days.

💼 15.4 Withdrawal Rules & Limits

Factor	Rule/Limit
Minimum Withdrawal	$10 (varies by country and method)
Maximum Per Transaction	$1,000–$5,000 (depending on region/account type)

Frequency	Daily withdrawals allowed (up to 1–3x/day in some areas)
Processing Time	1–5 business days (can be longer during holidays)
Currency Exchange Fees	May apply if withdrawing in a different currency
Tax Withholding	TikTok may withhold a portion for tax purposes

---

15.5 Withdrawal Methods Compared

Method	Speed	Fees	Requires Verification?	Recommended For
PayPal	1–3 business days	Low to none	Yes	Most creators globally
Bank Transfer	3–10 business days	Varies by bank	Yes	Business accounts or high volume
TikTok Wallet	Instant (in beta)	Internal use only	Yes	In-app purchases only

---

15.6 Common Issues & Solutions

Issue	Cause	Solution
Withdrawal button greyed out	Below minimum threshold	Wait until balance exceeds $10

"Account verification failed"	Wrong PayPal or bank info	Re-enter and re-verify with correct data
Delay in funds appearing	Processing or system backlog	Wait 5–10 business days; check TikTok Help
Withheld earnings	Account under investigation or flagged	Check for guideline violations or open support ticket
Amount less than expected	Currency exchange or transaction fees	Check breakdown in TikTok Studio > Earnings

---

📱 15.7 Tracking Your Cash Flow

To monitor your full income history:

- Go to **TikTok Studio > Earnings**
- Filter by:

  - Date range (7-day, 28-day, custom)
  - Type of income (Creator Rewards, LIVE, Shop)

- Export income records for tax tracking or financial planning

💡 Use this to estimate monthly or quarterly income and plan your creator schedule accordingly.

📓 15.8 Legal & Tax Considerations

TikTok earnings count as **self-employed income** in most countries. You may be responsible for:

- Declaring TikTok income in your tax filings
- Paying self-employment or creator tax (varies by region)
- Keeping detailed records of:

  - **Withdrawals**
  - **1099/K tax forms (U.S.)**
  - **Payout confirmations**

■ Always consult a tax professional or financial advisor, especially if you're earning regularly or at scale.

💡 15.9 Pro Tips for Smoother Payouts

- **Link your PayPal early** — even before reaching $10
- **Avoid changing your payout method too often**
- **Plan withdrawals before holidays** when banking systems slow down
- If you go **LIVE often**, consider batching withdrawals weekly for better financial planning
- Use **TikTok Studio reports** for budgeting, savings, and reinvestment

---

📓 Summary: TikTok Cash-Out Essentials

Step	What to Do
Earn Diamonds	Host LIVE sessions and receive gifts
Track Balance	Profile → Settings → Balance → LIVE Gifts
Link PayPal or Bank	Complete identity verification and payment info setup
Withdraw Funds	Select "Withdraw" and confirm your details
Review History	Monitor earnings via TikTok Studio → Earnings Tab
Report Issues	Use Help Center if payout fails or is delayed

With this knowledge, you now have full control over your TikTok income flow. Whether you're a casual gifter turned creator, a daily LIVE host, or an affiliate seller, your earnings are **yours to claim — professionally and confidently**.

Chapter 16: TikTok Promote Tools – Boosting Your Reach with Ads & Promotions

"Going viral is great. Going strategic is better."

While organic content can take you far on TikTok, sometimes you want to give your best posts a **targeted push** — especially if you're promoting a business, launching a product, building a brand, or just starting out. That's where TikTok's **Promote tool** comes in.

TikTok Promote is the platform's in-app advertising solution for creators, influencers, and small business owners who want to **boost videos, increase reach, drive traffic, or grow their audience** — all without needing advanced ad experience.

This chapter covers:

- What TikTok Promote is and how it works
- Step-by-step guide to setting up a promotion
- Budgeting, targeting, and choosing goals
- Promotion analytics and performance tips
- When to use Promote vs. organic growth

📢 16.1 What Is TikTok Promote?

TikTok Promote is a feature within the app that allows you to **turn any public video into a promoted post**, reaching more viewers than your normal organic traffic.

You can use Promote to:

- Gain more **followers**
- Get more **video views**
- Drive traffic to your **website or TikTok Shop**
  Boost **LIVE attendance**
- Highlight **events, services, or campaigns**

📌 *Promote is ideal for creators who want growth without investing in full TikTok Ads Manager campaigns.*

● 16.2 How to Access TikTok Promote

Option 1: From Your Video

1. Go to the TikTok video you want to promote
2. Tap the **"•••" (more options)** button
3. Tap **Promote**
4. Follow the setup flow

Option 2: From Creator Tools

1. Go to **Profile > ☰ > Creator Tools > Promote**
2. Choose a post from your video list
3. Set your promotion preferences

● *Only public videos (not private or restricted) are eligible for promotion.*

🔧 16.3 Setting Up a Promotion: Step-by-Step

◆ Step 1: Choose Your Goal

TikTok lets you pick what you want the promotion to achieve:

Goal Type	Best For
More Views	Boosting visibility, virality
More Followers	Building long-term audience
Website Visits	Driving traffic to external links
TikTok Shop Views	Selling products or affiliate items
LIVE Boost	Driving real-time viewers to your stream

- ♦ Step 2: Select Your Audience

You have two options:

- **Automatic (Recommended)** – TikTok selects a broad but optimized audience

- **Custom** – You define:

    - **Location**
    - **Gender**
    - **Age range**
    - **Interests** (e.g., Beauty, Tech, Gaming, Fitness)

  🧠 *If you're targeting a niche, use Custom. For general visibility, Automatic works well.*

- ♦ Step 3: Set Budget & Duration

Option	Details
Daily Budget	Minimum: ~$5 USD/day (depending on region)
Duration	1 to 7 days per promotion
Estimated Reach	TikTok will show projected views based on budget

You can **adjust or cancel** your campaign at any time during the run.

- ♦ Step 4: Payment & Launch

- Pay via **TikTok Promote Balance** or **linked credit card**
- Tap **Start Promotion**
- Monitor performance live within **Creator Tools > Promote**

■ 16.4 Tracking Your Promote Performance

In the Promote dashboard, you'll see:

- Total spend
- Impressions (how many people saw it)
- Views
- Likes, shares, and comments
- Follower conversions (if applicable)
- Clicks to external link (if used)

You can pause, extend, or duplicate a campaign based on performance.

> ■ *Use this data to compare promoted vs. organic reach — and decide which types of content to boost in the future.*

● 16.5 When to Use Promote (and When Not To)

■ Promote Is Ideal For:

- Product launches
- Events or LIVE countdowns
- Service ads or offers
- Building authority on niche topics
- Boosting posts with great performance potential

✘ Avoid Using Promote When:

- The video is underperforming organically
- It includes copyrighted music or muted sections
- You don't have a clear CTA (call to action)
- It's time-sensitive content that's already past relevance

> ● *Promoting a weak video won't magically make it go viral — quality still matters first.*

■ 16.6 Promote + TikTok Shop Strategy

Creators promoting **TikTok Shop items** can:

- Tag products in a video
- Use Promote to drive **traffic to product pages**
- Earn both **affiliate commission** and video rewards

Tip:

- Use product demos, reactions, or tutorials
- Boost them using Promote with a goal set to "More Views" or "Shop Visits"

16.7 Promote vs. TikTok Ads Manager

Feature	Promote Tool	TikTok Ads Manager
Ease of Use	Very simple (in-app, no setup)	Advanced (dashboard-based)
Custom Targeting	Basic demographic + interests	Full-funnel targeting options
Analytics	Light reporting	In-depth tracking + pixel
Budget Flexibility	Low entry ($5–10)	Medium to high budget
Best For	Creators, solopreneurs	Brands, agencies, large shops

Use Promote for fast, simple boosts — use Ads Manager when scaling across regions or running full campaigns.

16.8 Best Practices for TikTok Promote Success

- **Promote high-retention videos**, not random posts
- Add a clear **hook + CTA** ("Check this out," "Link in bio," etc.)
- Use **closed captions** for clarity across regions
- Choose **custom audiences** if targeting niche users or industries
- **Monitor comments** during the promotion — high engagement improves performance

---

■ 16.9 Can You Promote the Same Video Multiple Times?

Yes!

You can:

- Run **back-to-back campaigns**
- Test **different audience targets** or goals for the same video
- Promote a video once per **goal type** (e.g., views + followers separately)

This is great for **A/B testing** content formats and hooks.

▌ Summary: TikTok Promote Essentials

Feature	Purpose	Pro Tip
Promote Tool	Boost any TikTok video	Use with videos already performing well
Audience Targeting	Custom or automatic	Match to your niche or goal
Budgeting	Starts around $5/day	Higher spend = broader reach
Use Cases	Follower growth, product sales, LIVE views	Promote with a CTA in the video
Reporting	Track impressions, conversions, ROI	Use data to refine content strategy

---

Used wisely, Promote is a powerful tool — not just for influencers, but for **coaches, educators, musicians, small brands, and creative professionals** looking to make an impact fast.

It bridges the gap between great content and *guaranteed visibility*.

Chapter 17: TikTok Content Planning, niche selection – Calendars, Hooks & Posting Routines

"Inspiration is your spark. Planning is your fuel."

Posting randomly might help you get discovered once...
But *planning* helps you build **trust**, **momentum**, and **consistent growth**.

The most successful creators — big or small — aren't just creative. They're **organized**.

This chapter shows you how to:

- Design a **repeatable content system**
- Craft a personalized **content calendar**
- Build **scroll-stopping hooks**
- Develop a weekly/monthly **posting routine**
- Plan for **long-term growth** without burnout

■ 17.1 The Purpose of a TikTok Content Strategy

A content strategy is like a GPS — it tells your creativity where to go.

Here's why you need one:

- ■ **The algorithm favors consistency** — planned creators win
- ⧗ It saves time — no more "what should I post today?" stress
- ● It prevents burnout — you spread your energy wisely
- ● It aligns your content with your goals (growth, sales, trust, etc.

📌 Without a plan, you're guessing. With one, you're building.

■ 17.2 Building Your Content Calendar From Scratch

You don't need a fancy app — just a structure that works for *you*.

■ Step 1: Define Your Weekly Posting Frequency

Posting Goal	Recommended Frequency

Rapid Growth	1–2 posts **per day**
Balanced Growth	4–6 posts per **week**
Passive Presence	2–3 posts per **week**

▲ Start with what's sustainable, not what's impressive.

◼ Step 2: Define Your "Content Pillars"

Think of these as **content categories or series** you'll rotate through. Most top creators have 3–5 recurring styles, formats, or topics.

Examples of Content Pillars:

Type	Examples
Teach	Tips, hacks, breakdowns, tutorials
Entertain	Skits, trends, challenges, comedic POVs
Relate	"POV" content, rants, memes, niche humor
Sell	Product demos, before/after, TikTok Shop
Build Trust	Storytime, personal experience, behind-the-scenes
React	Duets, stitches, green screen, hot takes

Your Pillar Combo Might Look Like:

- Monday: Quick Tip
- Wednesday: Relatable POV
- Friday: Product Plug
- Sunday: Storytime or Reaction

■ Step 3: Create Your Weekly/Master Content Planner

Here's a simple layout (use Notion, Google Sheets, Trello, or a whiteboard):

Date	Content Type	Topic	Hook/Opening Line	Call to Action (CTA)	Status
Mon	Tutorial	"3 ways to style a silk scarf"	"Don't waste your scarves…"	"Follow for more outfit tips"	Drafted
Tue	POV	"Introvert at a party"	"POV: You regret showing up"	"Comment if this is you"	Filmed
Wed	Product Demo	"TikTok Shop LED Light"	"Wait for the glow-up…"	"Link in bio, limited stock"	Scheduled
Sat	Storytime	"My first viral moment"	"Here's how I got 500k views"	"What would you have done?"	Posted

---

🎧 17.3 Crafting Powerful Hooks That Keep People Watching

Your **hook** is the first 0.5–2 seconds — the moment that determines if someone scrolls or stays.

🔥 Types of Hook Styles:

Hook Type	Examples

Shock/Intrigue	"You're not supposed to see this, but…"
Confession	"Okay… I've never told anyone this before."
Command	"Stop scrolling — you need to hear this."
POV/Relatable	"POV: You're 30, single, and your plants are your babies."
Mystery Setup	"This is the biggest mistake I made last year."
Comparison	"$10 skincare vs $100 skincare — worth it?"
Process/Reveal	"Watch this room go from basic to beautiful…"

👍 Try writing 3 hooks per idea before choosing the best one.

Visual hook tips:

- Add **text overlays** with high contrast
- Use **facial expressions or props** immediately
- Begin mid-action (open a box, react to something)
- Include a **visual question** ("Can you guess what happens next?")

⏰ 17.4 Best Times to Post (and How to Find Yours)

There's no "universal" best time — but **TikTok's analytics** can help you discover yours.

How to Check:

1. Go to **TikTok Studio > Analytics > Followers**
2. Scroll down to **Follower Activity**
3. Note the hours/days when your followers are most active

Suggested Default Time Slots (if you're unsure):

- 9–11 AM (Morning break scrolls)
- 6–9 PM (Post-work relaxation time)
- Weekends: Late morning & evening

Consistency in your posting time helps TikTok's algorithm learn your pattern and audience behavior.

17.5 Structuring a Weekly Content Flow (That Builds Momentum)

Here's a proven weekly rhythm many creators use:

Example: 5-Day Posting Plan

Day	Content Type	Goal
Monday	Relatable POV	Reach / Shareability
Tuesday	Quick Tip / Teach	Authority / Value
Wednesday	Product Plug / CTA	Sales / Monetization
Friday	Skit / Trend	FYP / Community Growth
Sunday	Storytime / Personal	Trust / Emotional connection

Every post should serve at least ONE of these 3 purposes:

1. Attract (new viewers)

2. Nurture (existing audience)

3. Convert (into followers, sales, or engagement)

■ 17.6 Batch Filming, Drafting, and Scheduling

Batch creation is the #1 time-saving hack for TikTok.

- Record **3–5 videos at once**
- Use outfit changes or switch backgrounds for variety
  Keep drafts in TikTok or CapCut to edit later
- Schedule using **TikTok Studio (desktop)** for Business/Creator accounts

💡 *Use TikTok's built-in draft and scheduling features for up to 10 days in advance.*

⚙ 17.7 Helpful Tools for Planning & Execution

Tool	Function	Why Use It
Notion	Calendar + task manager	Easy to customize, visual boards
CapCut	Video editing for TikTok (owned by ByteDance)	Fast, mobile-friendly, TikTok-integrated
TikTok Studio	Drafts, scheduling, analytics	Official performance tracking
Trello	Kanban-style idea organization	Good for planning ahead and delegating
Airtable	Content database with tags	Ideal for high-volume creators & brands

---

🗣 17.8 Advanced Tip: Create a "Content Engine"

Here's how to keep content flowing without running out of ideas:

1. **Track repeatable formats** – e.g., "Text Conversations," "3 Mistakes," "Reacting to Comments"
2. Build a **"Quick Ideas" vault** – Notes app, voice memos, or a whiteboard

3. Use the **80/20 Rule** – 80% value or entertainment, 20% promotion
4. Review your **top 10 posts monthly** – See what to recycle, remix, or update

---

🌱 17.9 Avoiding Burnout: Sustainable Creation

Being consistent ≠ being online 24/7.

Here's how to stay productive without exhausting yourself:

- Set **boundaries** for screen time and posting windows
- Pre-film when energy is high, rest when it's not
- Reuse content: turn one LIVE into 5 short clips
- Rotate formats: one day skits, another just captions on B-roll
- Don't chase every trend — filter for what aligns

   ✦ *Your creativity thrives when your energy is protected.*

📓 Understanding Creator Search Insights on TikTok

What It's All About & Why It Matters

Creator Search Insights is a tool within TikTok that helps content creators stay ahead of the game by showing what topics people are actively searching for on the platform. Think of it as your personal content radar—it helps you:

- Discover trending topics.
- Identify content gaps (topics people want but can't find).
- Track how well your content performs in search results.

🚀 Why Is It Important?

If you're trying to grow on TikTok, you can't just post randomly and hope for virality. **Creator Search Insights gives you direction**. You can:

- Create smarter, search-driven content.
- Post with confidence knowing the topic has demand.
- Gain insights on what your followers are interested in.

🔍 How to Access Creator Search Insights

1. Open the TikTok app.
2. Tap the **Search icon** at the top.

3. Type "**creator search insights**" into the bar.
4. Tap **View** at the top of the results.
5. To learn more, tap the **... (More options)** button at the top right, then tap **Help**.

🔍 Exploring Popular Search Topics

You can explore what people are searching for, including hot trends or topics lacking content (content gaps).

How to Use It:

1. Open **Creator Search Insights**.
2. Use filters like:

   ○ **Content gap**: Topics people search for but aren't getting much content.
   ○ **Searches by followers** (if you have 1K+ followers): Shows what *your audience* is into.

3. Tap on a topic to view:

   ○ Its popularity
   ○ Related videos
   ○ Related searches

■ How to Use Search Analytics

Once you've posted content based on a trend, track how it's doing!

To View Analytics:

1. Go to **Creator Search Insights**.
2. Tap **Search analytics**.
3. Choose:
   ○ **All posts**: To see overall performance.
   ○ **Inspired posts**: Content you made from Search Insights topics.

4. Pick a date range (last 7 days, 14 days, or custom).
5. For deeper info, tap **Learn more** beside "All posts."

🎥 Creating a Post from Creator Search Insights

1. Inside **Creator Search Insights**, find a topic.
2. Tap **Create post** or **Create at the bottom**.
3. Film and post your video right away!

⭐ Saving Topics for Later

1. In **Creator Search Insights**, find a topic you want to remember.
2. Tap the **Favorites (⭐) button** next to the topic.
3. View your saved topics later by tapping **Favorites** at the top.

🔥 TikTok Niches That Work + Why They Work

Here's a list of popular and successful TikTok niches with short explanations:

Niche	Why It Works
Lifestyle & Aesthetics	People love relatable daily routines, room makeovers, and aesthetic visuals.
Fitness & Wellness	Workout routines, diet tips, and transformation journeys are super shareable and inspiring.
Beauty & Skincare	Tutorials, product reviews, and before/after results keep people hooked.
Educational/"Edutok"	Bite-sized tips (finance, history, tech, etc.) give value fast and build trust.
Fashion & Outfit Ideas	Try-on hauls and styling tips are visually engaging and trend-driven.

Comedy & Skits	Relatable humor and trends often go viral quickly.
Food & Recipes	Quick, tasty, or unique recipe content is extremely popular.
Motivation & Self-Improvement	Short, powerful messages resonate deeply and often get shared.
BookTok (Reading)	Book lovers create huge engagement around reviews, recommendations, and aesthetics.
DIY & Crafts	Viewers love watching things being made—from art to home décor.
Pet & Animal Content	Cute, funny, or wholesome animal videos are TikTok gold.
Gaming	Game tips, highlights, and reactions draw passionate fanbases.

✦ Final Tips

- Use the **Content gap filter** to find low-competition, high-demand topics.
- Save trending ideas you aren't ready to use yet.
- Always check your **Search analytics** to improve your future content strategy.
- Combine **your unique style** with trending topics to stand out.

Chapter 18: TikTok LIVE Creator Networks – Empowering Creators and Agencies

In the fast-paced world of digital content, platforms like TikTok are not only transforming how we consume media—they're reshaping how creators build careers. Among TikTok's most powerful innovations is **TikTok LIVE**, a feature that allows creators to connect with audiences in real-time. To help creators maximize this opportunity, TikTok established a specialized support system known as **TikTok LIVE Creator Networks**.

These networks are designed to foster sustainable creator growth through professional support, operational tools, and incentive programs. But beyond the creative guidance lies an equally important question: **Who pays for it all, and how does the system work?** This chapter breaks it down.

What Are TikTok LIVE Creator Networks?

TikTok LIVE Creator Networks are officially partnered agencies selected by TikTok to manage and support a roster of live-streaming creators. These agencies act as mentors, business consultants, and community managers—guiding creators through the challenges of growing a brand on TikTok LIVE.

They provide:

- Personalized coaching and strategy
- Access to incentive programs
- Product tools for stream management and analytics
- A structured ecosystem focused on positive and responsible content

These resources allow creators to focus on what they do best—creating—while agencies handle the operational backbone.

How Do Creator Networks Benefit Creators?

For creators, joining a Creator Network is like signing with a team of personal trainers—but for your content. Here's what they gain:

- **Incentive Programs**: Creators can join exclusive campaigns that reward consistency, growth, and creativity.
- **Operational Tools**: Dedicated dashboards help track engagement, revenue, and viewer behavior.
- **Coaching & Mentorship**: Agencies offer workshops, performance reviews, and creative feedback tailored to the creator's niche.

- **Positive Ecosystem**: Agencies help enforce TikTok's community guidelines and foster healthy streaming practices.

Perhaps most importantly: **these services are offered at no cost to creators.**

Who Pays the Agencies?

A common misconception is that creators have to pay for access to these services. In reality, **TikTok compensates the agencies directly**. Here's how it works:

- **TikTok funds Creator Networks** as part of its broader investment in creator success and platform health.
- Agencies may be paid a **base fee, a performance-based commission**, or through tiered milestone rewards based on creator achievements (like increased engagement or viewer retention).
- TikTok benefits by ensuring creators produce high-quality, engaging, and brand-safe content on its platform—making the investment worthwhile.

This model ensures that creators have access to professional support **without financial barriers**, which in turn encourages more authentic and creative broadcasting.

Do Creators Ever Pay?

In almost all cases, **creators do not pay to join or remain part of a Creator Network**. The goal is to make professional support accessible and remove friction from the growth process. However, in the future, some networks may offer optional premium services or partnerships outside of TikTok's direct framework—but these would be exceptions, not the rule.

Why It Works: A Win-Win-Win Ecosystem

The Creator Network model is a smart, sustainable system where everyone benefits:

- **Creators** get free tools, mentorship, and incentives to help them grow.
- **Agencies** receive compensation from TikTok and build their reputations as industry leaders.
- **TikTok** boosts creator success and keeps the LIVE ecosystem healthy and engaging for viewers.

This structure not only fuels content creation but also professionalizes the creator economy in a way that mirrors talent agencies in traditional media.

Final Thoughts

TikTok LIVE Creator Networks represent a new era of platform-supported content creation. By investing directly in agency-led mentorship and providing accessible resources to creators, TikTok is laying the groundwork for long-term digital careers.

Whether you're a creator looking to go LIVE with confidence or an agency eager to empower the next wave of influencers, TikTok's Creator Network program offers a smart, scalable way to succeed in the live-streaming space.

Chapter 19: Elevating Your Live Broadcasts — Mastering TikTok Live Studio and TikFinify Integration

In today's content-driven landscape, live streaming has evolved into a dynamic and immersive experience that blends entertainment, interaction, and real-time feedback. TikTok, one of the world's leading social platforms, has taken live content to the next level with **TikTok Live Studio**. When combined with **TikFinify**, a robust enhancement and analytics tool, the potential for professional-grade broadcasting becomes unparalleled. This chapter will serve as your ultimate guide to setting up, optimizing, and mastering these two tools to supercharge your live broadcasts.

---

1. Understanding TikTok Live Studio and TikFinify

TikTok Live Studio: The Control Center

TikTok Live Studio is TikTok's official desktop application that allows content creators to live stream using their PC setup. Unlike mobile live streaming, TikTok Live Studio provides:

- **Scene and Source Management**: Switch between webcams, gameplay, images, and media files.
- **Custom Layouts**: Create personalized layouts with text overlays, background images, and borders.
- **Real-Time Monitoring**: Track stream performance, monitor chat, and manage engagement.
- **Professional Audio/Video Input**: Use high-quality microphones, audio mixers, DSLR cameras, and capture cards.

TikFinify: The Enhancement Layer

TikFinify is an auxiliary platform that integrates seamlessly with TikTok Live Studio. It's designed to:

- Provide **in-depth analytics** on viewer behavior and engagement.
- Offer **interactive widgets** such as polls, Q&A, and donation alerts.
- Enable **custom overlay designs** and animations.
- Track **real-time monetization**, including virtual gifts and donations.
- Offer **automated moderation** tools to maintain a safe chat environment.

Together, they form a powerful toolkit for creators looking to produce immersive, data-driven live broadcasts.

---

2. System Requirements and Initial Setup

Hardware and Software Requirements

To run TikTok Live Studio and TikFinify smoothly, your system should meet the following specifications:

- **OS**: Windows 10 or later (64-bit)
- **Processor**: Intel Core i5 or AMD Ryzen 5 minimum
- **RAM**: 8GB (16GB recommended)
- **GPU**: Dedicated graphics card (NVIDIA or AMD)
- **Internet**: Minimum 5 Mbps upload speed (10 Mbps+ for 1080p or multi-camera)

Account Requirements

- **TikTok Account**: You must have access to TikTok Live, which typically requires:

  - At least 1,000 followers
  - Account in good standing
  - Age over 18 (for gifting and monetization)

- **TikFinify Account**: Sign up on the official TikFinify website. Some features may be premium.

3. Installing TikTok Live Studio

Step-by-Step Installation

1. **Download** TikTok Live Studio from the official TikTok creator tools portal.
2. **Install** the application by running the .exe file.
3. **Log In** with your TikTok credentials.
4. **Grant Access** to your webcam and microphone.

Initial Configuration

- Set up your camera and microphone.
- Select the default video resolution (720p or 1080p).
- Create your first scene layout using available sources.

---

4. Installing and Launching TikFinify

Step-by-Step Installation

1. **Visit** the TikFinify website.
2. **Download** the installer for your OS.

3. **Run** the installer and follow setup instructions.
4. **Create/Login** to your TikFinify account.

Connecting to TikTok Live Studio

- Launch TikFinify.
- Open TikTok Live Studio.
- TikFinify should auto-detect and prompt to connect.
- If not, manually enter stream key or sync via settings.

5. Configuring Your Stream

TikTok Live Studio Configuration

- **Title and Description**: Use engaging, keyword-optimized titles.

- **Stream Settings**:

  - Resolution: 1080p or 720p
  - Bitrate: 2500–5000 Kbps
  - Frame Rate: 30 or 60 FPS

- **Audio Setup**:

  - Primary microphone
  - Audio filters (noise suppression, compressor)

- **Scenes and Sources**:

  - Webcams
  - Screen capture
  - Images and media
  - Text boxes

TikFinify Configuration

- **Overlay Manager**:

  - Add real-time widgets (e.g., alerts, counters)
  - Design your overlay theme

- **Monetization Tools**:

  - Enable donation tracking
  - Display top contributors or milestones

- **Engagement Tools**:

- ○ Enable live polls
- ○ Set up Q&A widgets

- **Moderation**:

  - ○ Set banned keywords
  - ○ Enable spam filters

6. Going Live with an Integrated Setup

Pre-Live Checklist

- Check all scene transitions
- Verify mic levels
- Preview overlays and alerts
- Test stream privately if possible

Starting the Stream

- Press "Go Live" in TikTok Live Studio
- Monitor analytics from TikFinify dashboard
- Respond to viewer interactions in real time

Stream Management

- Adjust scenes on-the-fly
- Monitor viewer engagement and comments
- Use TikFinify alerts to react to gifts or donations

7. Perks of Integration

Enhanced Analytics

- Real-time audience retention metrics
- Heatmaps for peak engagement moments
- Viewer behavior flow

Custom Overlays

- Real-time alerts for:
  - ○ Follows
  - ○ Donations
  - ○ Shares

- Branded frames and custom animations

Interactive Engagement

- Live polling and audience feedback
- Timed Q&A sessions
- Comment-triggered actions (e.g., emoji storm)

Monetization Tracking

- Virtual gift dashboard
- Daily/weekly/monthly revenue stats
- Celebration triggers for milestones (e.g., 100 viewers)

Community Moderation

- Auto-delete harmful comments
- Assign trusted viewers as moderators
- Highlight and pin good comments

8. Best Practices

Technical Best Practices

- Run a speed test before each stream
- Use wired Ethernet for maximum stability
- Close background applications

Content Best Practices

- Plan your stream with segments
- Use transitions to maintain viewer interest
- Acknowledge and thank supporters

Post-Stream Actions

- Review TikFinify analytics
- Clip highlights for TikTok or YouTube
- Survey your audience for feedback

9. Final Thoughts

Combining TikTok Live Studio with TikFinify creates a powerful, all-in-one live streaming powerhouse that elevates content quality, viewer engagement, and monetization potential. Whether you're a gaming creator, educator, artist, or lifestyle influencer, mastering this integration will position you for growth and success in the increasingly competitive world of live broadcasting.

Experiment with new features, analyze performance regularly, and continue iterating to create impactful, high-quality live streams that stand out on TikTok.

Chapter 20: Navigating TikTok's Community Guidelines

TikTok isn't just a social platform—it's a shared digital space. With over a billion users, TikTok's primary concern is fostering a community built on **safety, respect, and dignity**. The updated **Community Guidelines** (released April 17, 2024, effective May 17, 2024) set clear expectations for content creators. Violations can lead to demonetization, content suppression, or permanent bans. Understanding what's off-limits isn't just smart—it's essential.

The Pillars of TikTok's Safety Policy

At the core of TikTok's approach are **physical and psychological safety**, **respectful discourse**, and **inclusion**. Users are encouraged to express themselves, but not at the expense of others' safety or dignity.

Let's break down the key categories TikTok moderates under its guidelines:

---

1. Violent and Criminal Behavior

TikTok prohibits:

- Threats of violence or inciting violence
- Promotion of criminal activity
- Display or use of weapons, including firearms (even if they are not real or owned by the user)
- Graphic imagery related to past injuries

Even seemingly harmless content like a photo of an old scar could fall afoul of these rules. TikTok will report credible threats to human life to law enforcement.

---

2. Hate Speech and Hateful Behavior

This is one of the strictest areas. TikTok bans content that:

- Attacks or demeans protected groups
- Promotes hateful ideologies like white supremacy or anti-LGBTQ+ rhetoric
- Uses slurs, even in coded or indirect ways

Protected attributes include (but aren't limited to): race, ethnicity, gender identity, religion, disability, and sexual orientation. Deadnaming and misgendering fall under this rule.

Even indirect mockery or stereotypes can make content **FYF-ineligible** (For You Feed). That means even if content isn't removed, it may be suppressed.

3. Violent and Hateful Organizations

TikTok does not permit:

- Promoting or quoting violent extremist or hate groups
- Providing material support (e.g., selling merch, recruiting) for such groups
- Amplifying hate figures, even passively

Important: Even referencing these organizations must clearly indicate condemnation or educational intent.

4. Abuse: Youth and Adults

No content may:

- Promote or depict youth sexual exploitation or abuse
- Show or imply grooming, sextortion, or harassment
- Display or encourage adult abuse (physical, sexual, or emotional)
- Include unsolicited or non-consensual imagery (even jokes)

Survivors **can** share their stories—as long as they avoid explicit or graphic details.

5. Human Trafficking and Smuggling

TikTok prohibits:

- Any coordination or promotion of human trafficking or smuggling
- Instructions or services related to document fraud or illegal migration

However, content that shares a **migrant's journey or survivor story** (without glamorizing or including illegal activity) is allowed.

6. Harassment and Bullying

You may not:

- Target someone based on appearance, intelligence, health, or personal tragedy
- Encourage others to attack or mass report someone (coordinated harassment)
- Share private information (doxxing) or threaten to do so

Criticism of content is fine—but personal attacks are not.

The Don'ts: Common Mistakes Creators Make

TikTok is very clear about certain "gray area" violations. Here's what you **shouldn't** do—even if you think it's harmless:

- Use slurs, even if you're part of the group being referenced (e.g., using the word "gay" may still be flagged)
- Post firearms—even fake or legally owned ones
- Ask people to "click the OF link in bio," even jokingly
- Use violent or sensitive words in captions, even if it's in a figurative or sarcastic context
- Show old injuries or scars
- Display personal ID cards—even if it's your own

Restricted Words and Recommended Replacements

Below is a guide to commonly flagged words and safer alternatives for creators:

Restricted Word/Phrase	Suggested Alternative
Kill / Killing	Take down / Defeat / Eliminate (in games)
Gun / Firearm	Pew pew / Tool / Prop (if fictional)
Midget	Little person / Person of short stature
Gay (as a label)	LGBTQ+ / Queer community (context-sensitive)
OF / OnlyFans	Link in bio (avoid direct callouts or jokes)
Click my OF link	"Link for 18+ in bio" (even this is risky)

Injury photo	"Throwback to tough times" (without image)
Racial Slurs	Avoid entirely, even when quoting or reclaiming
Deadnaming / Misgendering	Use chosen name and pronouns
Doxxing / ID reveal	Never show personal information
Pedophilia references	Use "inappropriate behavior" or "abuse"

Final Thoughts: Create with Care

TikTok is giving creators a platform and a responsibility. If your content aims to **educate, entertain, or inspire**, then staying aligned with these guidelines should feel like second nature. Think before you post. Read the room. And if you're ever in doubt—don't hit upload.

TikTok isn't here to silence voices. It's here to make sure every voice is heard **safely**.

Tik Tok Gifter Level Up

Level	Coin		Level	Coin
LV.1	1		LV.21	39,600
LV.2	8		LV.22	54,600
LV.3	18		LV.23	75,800
LV.4	34		LV.24	105,000
LV.5	56		LV.25	144,000
LV.6	90		LV.26	196,000
LV.7	140		LV.27	265,000
LV.8	220		LV.28	357,000
LV.9	340		LV.29	478,000
LV.10	530		LV.30	637,000
LV.11	820		LV.31	845,000
LV.12	1,260		LV.32	1,120,000
LV.13	1,920		LV.33	1,470,000
LV.14	2,840		LV.34	1,920,000
LV.15	4,340		LV.35	2,500,000
LV.16	6,420		LV.36	3,230,000
LV.17	9,280		LV.37	4,180,000
LV.18	13,500		LV.38	5,430,000
LV.19	19,400		LV.39	6,890,000
LV.20	27,600		LV 40	8,780,000
LV.45	27,900.000		LV 50	80,000.000

Tiktok Gifter Level Up

Level	Cumulative Coins	Coins to Next Level	Approximate USD	Level	Cumulative Coins	Coins to Next Level	Approximate USD
1	1	7	$0.01	26	196000	69,000	$2,607.84
2	8	10	$0.11	27	265000	92,000	$3,525.27
3	18	16	$0.24	28	357000	121,000	$4,747.89
4	34	22	$0.45	29	478000	159,000	$6,351.74
5	56	34	$0.75	30	637000	208,000	$8,466.21
6	90	50	$1.20	31	845000	275,000	$11,243.00
7	140	80	$1.86	32	1120000	350,000	$14,896.00
8	220	120	$2.93	33	1470000	450,000	$19,551.00
9	340	190	$4.52	34	1920000	580,000	$25,536.00
10	530	290	$7.05	35	2500000	730,000	$33,250.00
11	820	440	$10.93	36	3230000	950,000	$42,959.00
12	1,260	660	$16.76	37	4,180,000	1,200,000	$55,592.00
13	1,920	920	$25.54	38	5,380,000	1,510,000	$71,554.00
14	2,840	1,500	$37.77	39	6,890,000	1,890,000	$91,637.00
15	4,340	2,080	$57.74	40	8,780,000	2,420,000	$116,774.00
16	6,420	2,860	$85.39	41	11,200,000	2,900,000	$149,040.00
17	9,280	4,070	$123.42	42	14,100,000	3,700,000	$187,533.00
18	13,350	6,050	$177.56	43	17,800,000	4,500,000	$236,740.00
19	19,400	8,400	$258.02	44	22,300,000	7,700,000	$296,590.00
20	27,800	11,800	$369.74	45	30,000,000	4,700,000	$399,000.00
21	39,600	15,000	$526.68	46	34,700,000	12,800,000	$461,510.00
22	54,600	21,200	$726.18	47	47,500,000	18,200,000	$632,750.00
23	75,800	29,200	$1,008.14	48	65,700,000	9,300,000	$874,810.00
24	105,000	39,000	$1,397.25	49	75,000,000	22,500,000	$998,750.00
25	144,000	52,000	$1,916.52	50	97,500,000	—	$1,297,750.00

www.ingramcontent.com/pod-product-compliance
Lightning Source LLC
LaVergne TN
LVHW060144070326
832902LV00018B/2952